Sourcebook for Bibliographic Instruction

Katherine Branch, Chair
Sourcebook for Bibliographic Instruction Task Force

Carolyn Dusenbury
Consulting Editor

Sourcebook for Bibliographic Instruction Task Force
Barbara Conant
Cynthia Roberts
Kimberly Spyers-Duran

Bibliographic Instruction Section
Association of College and Research Libraries
A Division of the American Library Association
1993

Published by the Association of College and Research Libraries
A Division of the American Library Association
50 East Huron Street
Chicago, IL 60611-7295

ASSOCIATION OF

COLLEGE

& RESEARCH

LIBRARIES

ISBN: 0-8389-7673-5

This publication is printed on recycled paper.

Acknowledgements

As with any cooperative, all-volunteer project, many individuals worked very hard to bring this book into print. The clear , readable layout of this publication is entirely due to the careful, dedicated, and time-consuming work of Louise News, administrative assistant at Catonsville Community College Library, and Cynthia Roberts, Collection Development Librarian at Catonsville.

The chair of the Sourcebook Editorial Board would like to give special thanks to Carolyn Dusenbury, the consulting editor for the book, for her tact, faith, and good humor during the editing process. The Task Force for the Sourcebook for Bibliographic Instruction is very grateful for the support and encouragement of the chairs of the Bibliographic Instruction Section during the period in which the book was planned, written and edited: Cerise Oberman (1989/90), Betsy Wilson (1990/91), Mary Ellen Litzinger (1991/92), and Sharon Mader (1992/93), and to Claudette Hagle, the BIS Executive Committee liaison to the Task Force.

The Task Force would also like to acknowledge the original members of the BIS Task Force for Needs Assessment of a Bibliographic Instruction Section's Librarian's Handbook: Rae Haws, Sandra Rosenstock, Tom Zogg, and Diane Zwemer. We also acknowledge the work of Donna Hitchings, a member of the Task Force for the Sourcebook for Bibliographic Instruction from 1990 through 1991.

Table of Contents

Introduction

Sourcebook for Bibliographic Instruction

The purpose of this book is to provide direction and guidance in establishing and maintaining bibliographic instruction (BI) programs. The *Sourcebook* is intended to be a working, desktop tool for new bibliographic instruction librarians. Experienced bibliographic instruction librarians should find the book useful in modifying or re-examining existing programs. Library school students and faculty may find the *Sourcebook* helpful in library school courses on bibliographic instruction. Rather than being a lengthy comprehensive book, the Sourcebook provides an overview of bibliographic instruction and points readers to other sources of information, such as important publications, clearinghouses and associations.

It is particularly fitting that this book was completed fifteen years after the inception of the Bibliographic Instruction Section (BIS). Originally established in 1978 to "support quality higher education by promoting instruction in the access, evaluation, and utilization of information resources," (Handbook 1978) the Section has grown to over 3000 members. Through its programs, publications and activities, the Section strives to enhance the ability of academic and research bibliographic instruction librarians to effectively serve the library and information needs of current and potential library users. Within the past two years, the Section has published two other books which can serve as companion pieces to the *Sourcebook*: *Read This First: An Owner's Guide to the New Model Statement of Objectives for Academic Bibliographic Instruction* and *Learning to Teach*, which assists librarians in teaching other librarians to teach.

Using the Sourcebook

The *Sourcebook* is intended to be practical and easy-to-use, yet not overlook the theoretical underpinnings of the field of bibliographic instruction. In any field based on theory, there are differences of opinion about the usefulness of various theoretical constructs. The approach taken in the *Sourcebook* is to present all relevant viewpoints neutrally, omitting judgements about their relative value to the practitioner. This approach exposes the reader to more than one viewpoint, allowing them to read further about the theories that interest them or that are judged to be useful in their institutional setting.

Decisions about what to include in the *Sourcebook* were guided by asking what knowledge was essential for the new bibliographic instruction librarian. Five key topics were identified and authors solicited to contribute these chapters. The task force recognized that many topics, such as using newer instructional technologies, marketing BI programs and cultural diversity, were important to BI librarians. Authors were encouraged to either incorporate references to these topics into their chapters or to provide references to good readings on the topics.

The *Sourcebook* begins with a chapter, written by Lori Arp, highlighting the importance of understanding learning theory traditions and developments. This chapter also covers how and why to write objectives and discusses the relationship of learning theory to bibliographic instruction. The second chapter covers instructional systems design and is written by Mary Ellen Litzinger. The process of instructional systems design encourages the instructor to identify the instructional problem, design the solution, implement the solution, and evaluate the solution. Though other approaches to instruction might weigh the various components of instructional design differently or emphasize somewhat different components, instructional design provides a useful framework for carefully planning bibliographic instruction sessions. In the third chapter, Randy Hensley covers specific teaching methods, including factors such as the level of instruction needed and the factors to consider in selecting a particular teaching method. Some of the specific methods covered include course-related instruction, lecture, active learning, point-of-use, computer-assisted instruction and interactive multimedia. The fourth chapter, written by Mignon Adams, covers evaluation and its importance in bibliographic instruction. Types of evaluation, such as formative and summative evaluation, outcomes assessment, and qualitative evaluation are covered. Evaluation instruments such as observation, surveys, tests, questionnaires, and checklists are reviewed. In the last chapter, Esther Grassian discusses how to plan for, set up, and manage a bibliographic instruction program. Topics such as identifying the library's and BI program's goals, training BI instructors, publicizing BI programs, and garnering support for the program are addressed.

History of the Sourcebook

In 1979, the Bibliographic Instruction Section published the *Bibliographic Instruction Handbook*. The purpose of the *Handbook*, as stated in its introduction, was to "provide guidance in the development of instruction programs and stimulate discussion about bibliographic instruction within the profession" and to "provide leadership in the development of the concept of bibliographic instruction" (Handbook 1978). Compiled by the BIS Policy and Planning Committee, the *Handbook* was short, less than one hundred pages, and practical. Sections of the *Handbook* covered: guidelines for BI, a needs assessment checklist, administrative considerations, model statements for a BI program, timetable and objectives, an assessment of the pros and cons of various modes of instruction, a glossary, and a pathfinder.

The *Handbook* sold about 1200 copies, going out of print in 1987. Since that time, the American Library Association and BIS have continued to receive requests for the *Handbook*. One section of the *Handbook*, the model statement of objectives, was revised in 1988 and was the focus of the 1990 BIS program at the ALA Annual Conference. The model statement of objectives was also the focus of *Read This First*, mentioned above. In the summer of 1989, Cerise Oberman, the BIS chair, appointed a Task Force for Needs Assessment of a Bibliographic Instruction Section Librarians' Handbook to recommend whether the Handbook should be replaced. Task force members included Katherine Branch, Barbara Conant, Rae Haws, Cynthia Roberts, Sandra Rosenstock, Diane Zwemer, and Tom Zogg.

To determine whether the *Handbook* should be replaced this task force took a number of steps to assess the need for a replacement to the *Handbook*. These steps included: polling more than thirty bibliographic instruction leaders, publishing a questionnaire in three newsletters, contacting ALA publishing to determine the sales history of the *Handbook*, assessing the limitations of the then newly-published *LIRT Library Instruction Handbook*, discussing our opinions as task force members about replacing the *BI Handbook*, and compiling a bibliography of book-length works on BI to determine whether the need for such a *Handbook* was already met. The task force found that there was a strong need for a BIS sponsored publication directed at new bibliographic instruction librarians.

Many of the bibliographic instruction leaders polled by the task force stated that BIS should play a strong role in continuing to educate the new BI librarian by replacing the *Handbook*. The *Sourcebook* supports the BIS goals of contributing to the total professional development of bibliographic instruction librarians, enhancing the capability of bibliographic instruction programs and librarians to serve user needs, and promoting the interest of academic librarians involved in bibliographic instruction.

In a rapidly changing world that is fraught with social and economic problems, the role of the bibliographic instruction librarian in teaching how to open the doors to the world of knowledge has never been as important. Whether one refers to what we do as bibliographic instruction or information literacy, the importance of our work cannot be over-stated. We hope that the *Sourcebook* will help us do this work even better.

Chapter One

An Introduction to Learning Theory

Lori Arp
University of Colorado at Boulder

Research about how people learn has informed teaching practice and educational theory for decades in the American educational system. Recently, this focus has become especially important as reformers call for the development of a new type of worker, one who can respond, flexibly and dynamically, in the rapidly changing markets and political conditions existent in a global community. Educators are working to teach students how to think, and learn, and to translate these abilities to situations outside the traditional educational environment.

The rapid technological changes of the last decades exemplify how quickly both technology and methods of information retrieval can become obsolete. At the same time, the explosion of information sources and systems and their consequent complexity makes navigating this maze a difficult but crucial ability for success in any discipline. For the instruction librarian, these issues pose a difficult problem: on one hand, rapid change makes skills quickly obsolete; on the other, the need has never been greater to inform students of the methods and strategies of effective information access. Monitoring research on learning and its applications in educational theory and practice can help librarians clarify problems like this one.

Understanding learning theory is essential to providing good bibliographic instruction. Learning theory transforms not only what we teach but how we teach, for different theories suggest different teaching methods and approaches. As a discipline, the field of bibliographic instruction focuses more on applying various learning theories than on developing them. Most theories used have been drawn from the fields of educational psychology, psychology, and cognitive science. This chapter will survey both older and more recent views of learning which have been applied in bibliographic instruction, and provide a context in which to view them.

Overview of Learning Theory Traditions

Learning theory generally can be divided into two broad traditions: the behavioral theories and the cognitive theories. Behavioral theories originated in the early part of this century. They assume that knowledge can be broken into smaller units and that knowledge acquisition can be measured by changes in behavior. Behavioral theories also assume that the learner is a blank slate or an empty vessel into which knowledge can be poured. These approaches view knowledge as independent of thinking abilities and knowledge acquisition as an additive process. In other words, each separate piece of knowledge can be taught independently, "adding" the next to the last. Cognitive theories originated in the late 1970s and 1980s as a response to research results that could not be accounted for in behavioral theories. They assume that the learner actively interacts with the environment and that each learner creates knowledge which is unique. In this alternative view, knowledge is perceived as a holistic process, not as an additive process, and can only be learned by going back and forth between parts and wholes. Different instructional approaches result from behavioral and cognitive theories. Behavioral approaches are centered around the teacher and what the teacher teaches. Cognitive approaches are student-oriented and view the teacher as coach, modeler, or facilitator. An excellent overview of these two traditions is provided by Aluri and Reichel in "Learning Theories and Bibliographic Instruction" (Aluri and Reichel 1984).

Behavioral Theory and Educational Objectives

Behavioral theory is heavily based on the stimulus-response experiments of B.F. Skinner and on the assumption that external observation of changes in behavior can indicate that learning has occurred. Nancy Cole comments that "this conception of learning had the advantages of focusing quite clearly on the desired outcome (the behavior) and of suggesting specific instructional actions (e.g. reinforcement) that should be followed. The theories were well suited to the political times of increasing public concern that children were not learning to read, write, or perform basic arithmetic operations" (Cole 1990). Educational objectives were viewed in this theory as the method of planning and measuring behavior. A number of articles have articulated reasons why using objectives were viewed to be beneficial (Mager 1962). Generally, objectives are considered useful for selecting specific concepts to be taught, for evaluating the success of instruction, and for validating proposed direction. Beaubien *et al.* also describe several reasons why instructional objectives are useful to librarians and students (Beaubien 1982).

Educational objectives became well known in higher education with the publication of the *Taxonomy of Educational Objectives*, (Bloom 1956) developed under the direction of two committees chaired by Bloom and Krathwohl in 1956 and 1964 respectively, and by Mager's book on the form of objectives published in 1965. In the Taxonomy, the psychological bases of educational objectives were used to organize a set of general and specific categories that encompass all possible learning outcomes. The categories were arranged in a hierarchical order. The Taxonomy was based on the assumption that learning outcomes could be best described in terms of changes in performance by students and that the categories could be generalized across all content areas and age levels. The *Taxonomy* was divided into three areas:

> **The Cognitive domain** - Those objectives which look at thinking skills and emphasize intellectual outcomes;
> **The Affective domain** - Those objectives that emphasize feeling and emotion;
> **The Psychomotor domain** - Those objectives which emphasize motor skills.
> (This domain was never completed in the *Taxonomy* document.)

The cognitive and affective domains were then divided into categories. Hierarchies were established in each, organized from simple to complex, and from concrete to abstract. For example, the major categories of the cognitive domain are listed in Gronlund's *How to Write and Use Instructional Objectives* (Gronlund 1991). The categories of knowledge, comprehension and application were considered lower level cognitive outcomes. Higher level thinking skills were considered to be the areas of analysis, synthesis, and evaluation.

Robert Mager articulated the structure of a successful learning outcome (Mager 1962). He comments that a useful learning outcome should have the following characteristics:

1. **Performance**. The objective should state what the learner is expected to be able to do;
2. **Conditions**. The objective should state under what conditions performance is expected to occur;
3. **Criterion**. The objective should describe the quality or level of performance considered acceptable.

An example of an instructional objective which provides these characteristics is:

> Given a list of materials with call numbers and/or location symbols, a student can successfully retrieve all items on the list that are in the library that are properly shelved.

In the seventies, the literature reflects the development of statements of objectives in a number of disciplines and a further articulation of the "action verbs" to be utilized in writing objectives for each area of the cognitive and affective domains. Gronlund summarizes this activity in his book entitled *How to Write and Use Instructional Objectives* (Gronlund 1991).

Emergence of Cognitive Thinking and Learning

At the end of the 1970s, new and alternative theories of learning began to emerge. Some of these were driven by new experimental data in psychology, education, and linguistics which could not be accounted for by behavioral theories. Many psychologists and educators began to question the model of the student as an empty vessel into which knowledge could be poured. An alternative view has emerged which sees the learner as an active participant in the learning process who constructs knowledge and brings his or her own view of the world to this process.

Since Gagne's work on learning theory, it has been gradually accepted that the process of learning is a much more complex phenomenon than originally supposed. Cognitive theories focused initially on the importance of teaching concepts, and the way in which components create an interrelated whole. New thinking has taken this idea one step further. It is now believed that one must view the whole interaction in context, including the student's emotional state, background and view of the issue as well as the teacher's view and background. Unlike the behavioral view that learning is a private process, learning is viewed from this approach as a public process. Richard Paul comments that in this approach "authoritative answers are replaced by authorative standards for engagement in the communal process of inquiry" (Paul 1989). If this perspective is accepted, it transforms the manner in which instructional intervention occurs, for the teacher no longer becomes an "absolute authority", but is a participant in the learning process. Long lectures are replaced with active interactions, with the teacher as coach, modeler, and facilitator.

Initial cognitive theory focused on the development of schema theory and knowledge domains. Piaget initially developed schema theory (Gruen 1977), which suggests that the mind has a structure based on perceptions and experience. Similar patterns are incorporated into existing schema as new experiences are absorbed. Experience will transform the structure of schema. Along with schema, the acceptance of the idea that knowledge has separate domains is paramount. In this view, a domain is a specific body of knowledge or content area. In libraries, we often think of these as fields or disciplines. Each knowledge domain, then, may have its own schema or a number of schema depending on the individual's experiences or perceptions in that area. In this approach, learning is not accumulating knowledge, but a process of conceptual change in which the learner revises an existing cognitive model of the world. This requires active participation or processing by the learner. The term schema describes a cognitive structure for representing knowledge. Other terms which have similar meaning include mental models, scripts, or frames. An example of a schema might include the purpose of using an index, or having a mental model of an atom.

Important recent work has focused on the demonstrated difference between novice and expert knowledge as a way of understanding learning. According to Glaser, experts display:

- a coherence of what is known
- knowledge of domain-specific patterns or principles
- use of patterns and principles in problem solving
- recognition of situations and conditions for using knowledge
- highly efficient performance
- use of self regulating skills (i.e., metacognition or thinking about how you think) (Glaser 1984)

Novices do not display these traits.

The second issue listed above, whether thinking (and learning) is transferable from one domain to another, has been the cause of some controversy. Some experts (Ennis

1990; McPeck 1990) believe that higher order thinking skills, such as critical thinking, are transferable from one domain or discipline to another. Others believe that higher-order thinking skills are domain specific. This discussion is exemplified by the controversy common on university campuses over whether critical thinking can be taught as a separate course or needs to be integrated throughout the curriculum.

The literature of cognitive science as it relates to learning seems to be diverse and full of debate. It appears to be intrinsically tied to research on thinking and knowledge acquisition. There are even theories which are hybrids between behavioral and cognitive approaches. This confusion seems to revolve around what is termed "basic skills mastery" and "higher order thinking". Nancy Cole comments that basic skills are founded in behavioral psychology, whereas higher order skills are founded in philosophy and cognitive psychology (Cole 1990). Some individuals have even used behavioral approaches for "basic skills" and cognitive approaches for "higher order reasoning", switching traditions at will. Neither the behavioralists nor the cognitive scientists view this as valid and each has definitions and attitudes about these types of learning.

Many learning theories advocated in the 1980s tend to be individualistic in their views. Recently, Frances and Michael Jacobson have suggested the idea that different theories, in fact, illuminate different facets of the learning environment and may synergistically combine. In their article entitled, "Applying Current Cognitive Learning Theories to Bibliographic Instruction: A Case Study of End User Searching", (Jacobson and Jacobson 1992) the authors combine three important learning theories which reflect current themes in cognitive science and then suggest an application for instructional practice. The theories combined are:

1. **Mental Models Transformation**: This theory was inspired by studies of problem solving which revealed how experts use many schemas or models when reasoning in disciplines (domains). This approach assumes that students must frequently restructure or reorder their knowledge in order to understand complex issues (Jacobson and Jacobson 1992).
2. **Cognitive Flexibility Theory**: This theory is based on the assumption that oversimplification of complex knowledge contributes to learning failures of students. It suggests several instructional approaches to overcome the tendency to present complex instructional content in overly simplified and decontextualized ways. The theory uses case study as a teaching approach (Spiro 1987 and 1988).
3. **Situated Cognition**: This theory states that knowledge is learned within a social context that itself shapes thinking and learning. The social situation provides a framework for authentic activity as practiced by experts. Learning is a process that involves the internalization of social cognitive structures (Brown 1989).

Jacobson and Jacobson, among others, believe that the manner in which instructional intervention occurs is one of the most crucial aspects of applying and creating theory. Nickerson has summarized this beautifully. He says, "Teachers have a dual agenda: in each content area they must consider (1) which strategies students need in order to learn content and (2) how students can be helped to learn those strategies. The concept of strategic teaching is rich with meaning because it connotes teaching in a planful way, using certain instructional strategies that are believed to be effective in promoting understanding, and the teaching of strategies that students will find useful in learning and thinking" (Nickerson 1989).

Cognitive theories of learning, then, accept the viewpoint that learning is a complex process which cannot be divorced from the learner as an active participant in the process. They accept that experts have specific knowledge domains and that they create and have multiple mental models which are representative of that domain. They articulate the belief that situated learning is critical, i.e., that learning occurs in context. Finally, they advocate that the teacher is a participant and facilitator in the learning process rather than an absolute authority.

Application of Learning Theory to Bibliographic Instruction

The resurgence of interest in bibliographic instruction in the 1960s and 1970s as an almost grassroots movement in librarianship coincided with the large scale popularity of the use of objectives and learning outcomes. It is hardly surprising, then, that one of the first documents developed, once bibliographic instruction librarians organized, was a model statement of instructional objectives that looked at student performance. The document was originally published in the *Bibliographic Instruction Handbook*, the predecessor to this *Sourcebook*. The first Model Statement followed behavioral theory and had over 30 objectives designed to measure behavior. The focus of the Statement was also skill based. Each discrete component could be taught separately. For example, one objective listed is:

> "Given a map of the library, the student can correctly identify the location of the library's catalog and other holdings lists in a specified period of time."

In 1987, a new Model Statement was published. The revised document originally appeared in *College and Research Library News* and has been reprinted in *Read This First: An Owner's Guide to the New Model Statement* (Dusenbury 1991). This document was a bridge between behavioral and cognitive theories. It is an important document in the sense that it is one of the first times BIS officially recognized the importance of concepts and concept-based learning. It was never intended to imply that teaching concepts alone are sufficient, however. While the document is presented in the behavioral mode of objectives, it can be used in either theoretical tradition. It presents a framework for thinking about bibliographic instruction. It describes how information is identified and defined by experts, structured, intellectually accessed, and physically organized and accessed. It attempts to raise questions about what the conceptual content of bibliographic instruction could encompass. In this sense, it presents concepts and how they are interrelated, rather than providing skill-based objectives. There are no objectives listed which describe behavior. However, the model statement also has real drawbacks for each tradition. From the cognitive view, it is structured in a way that is teacher centered and too formula driven. From the behavioral view, it is too limited. The key verbs used are "understand" and "recognize". There are no objectives listed for the affective domain (Jacobovitz 1987), and the list does not follow Bloom's Educational Taxonomy in dividing lower-level and higher-level cognitive outcomes. Still, as it stands, it can serve as a broad overview of important concepts for cognitive theories' application. And with some additions, it can serve as a model document for behavioral applications as well. *Read This First* presents different traditions in which the Model Statement was used successfully. Perhaps this diversity reflects where we stand as a discipline in relating to learning theory.

Behavioral and cognitive theories of learning have also been applied in numerous articles about bibliographic instruction. For example, Aluri and Reichel have described some applications of cognitive theories (Aluri and Reichel 1984; Mellon 1980 and 1987). Baker and Sandore have discussed the use of analogy in relation to teaching the online catalog, and Oberman has described the importance of active learning and the use of analogy (Baker and Sandore 1987; Oberman 1991). Petrowski and Wilson have described the use of cooperative learning techniques (Petrowski and Wilson 1991). Finally, Jacobson and Jacobson have provided a theorical synthesis of their approach to learning within the library environment (Jacobson and Jacobson 1992).

Understanding Learning Theories

Learning about how people learn is not "too theoretical". Although the literature is diverse and rich, learning theory can have significant impact on even the 50-minute instruction session. Learning theory can transform what we teach, how we teach, and when we teach. To understand more about learning theory, the following steps are recommended:

1. First, read articles of learning theories which apply to bibliographic instruction. Many are listed at the end of this chapter. Most BI authors establish the context of the theory rather than jumping directly to pros and cons related to a particular theory.
2. Turn to original authors after you have established the context of a specific idea. Look first for review articles which set the context.
3. Try to highlight what certain theories will mean in terms of action by you or students in the classroom. For example, given certain theories, review when and at what point in instruction it may be appropriate to turn to case study or to use analogy.
4. While most theories have empirical evidence to support them at this time, there is no one way which is universally acknowledged as best. Don't be concerned about what is "best" in a given situation. Experiment to determine this and report your results.

Using Learning Theories

It is very difficult to suggest one path to follow when applying different learning theories. There are, however, some general statements which may be of use:

1. No matter what theory you follow, it is essential to conduct a needs analysis with the students targeted. How this is done will depend on the theory you are using. Behavioral theory might suggest using pre and post testing. Cognitive theory might suggest using cognitive style mapping as well as a variety of other techniques to determine learning style. Behavioral theory would focus primarily on the content issues of what the teacher desires to be learned. Cognitive theory would take into account socioeconomic issues, background, emotional state, and an individual's cognitive strengths and weaknesses.

2. All theories, including behavioral approaches, acknowledge the importance of teaching concepts. Cognitive theorists would warn against teaching concepts out of context, or as "rules". All theories seem to agree generally that concepts are not enough by themselves. Application must occur.

3. All theories acknowledge different teaching styles. Behavioral theory tends to work best in situations with predictable outcomes with well-structured knowledge using such techniques such as computer-assisted instruction and programmed instruction. Cognitive theories have very specific applications for when it is appropriate to use certain types of teaching methods such as collaborative learning, analogy, modeling of behavior, and case study, to use a few examples.

4. All theories acknowledge the importance of evaluating progress. Behavioral theorists believe learning is demonstrated through behavior. Cognitive theories accept other measures of learning as well and most apply a holistic approach to evaluation.

5. No theory accepts the premise that teaching by "instinct" is enough. Regardless of which theory you employ, you need to know why you are engaging students in a particular activity and what results can be expected.

The literature of learning theory is diverse, rich, and in development. New theories of learning are being suggested which will have an impact on how we teach and what we teach. As librarians, it is important for us to be aware of both newer and older theories of learning and to participate in experimenting with the resultant teaching methods suggested. By participating in the development and testing of theory, we can help inform both students and our colleagues and define the scope and direction of effective education in the future.

References

Aluri, Rao and Mary Reichel, "Learning Theories and Bibliographic Instruction." In *Bibliographic Instruction and the Learning Process: Theory, Style and Motivation,* edited by Carolyn Kirkendall, 15-25. Ann Arbor, Mich.: Pierian Press, 1984.

Beaubien, Anne K. et al. *Learning the Library.* New York: Bowker, 1982.

Bloom, B.S., ed. *Taxonomy of Educational Objectives: Handbook I, Cognitive .* New York: David C. McKay, 1956.

Brown, John Seely , Allan Collins and Paul Duguid, "Situated Cognition and the Culture of Learning." *Educational Researcher* 18 (January-February 1989): 32-42.

Cole, Nancy S. "Conceptions of Educational Achievement." *Educational Researcher* 19 (April 1990): 2.

Dusenbury, Carolyn, ed. *Read This First: An Owner's Guide to the New Model Statement of Objectives for Academic Bibliographic Instruction.* Chicago: Bibliographic Instruction Section, Association of College and Research Libraries, 1991.

Ennis, Robert H. "The Extent to Which Critical Thinking is Subject Specific: Further Clarification." *Educational Researcher* 19 (May 1990): 13.

Glaser, Robert. "Education and Thinking: the Role of Knowledge." *American Psychologist* 39 (1984): 93-104.

Glaser, Robert. "Cognitive and Environmental Perspectives on Assessing Achievement." in *Assessment in the Service of Learning: Proceedings of the 1987 ETS Invitational Conference .* Princeton: Educational Testing Service, 1988.

Gronlund, Norman E. *How to Write and Use Instructional Objectives.* New York: Macmillan, 1991.

Gruen, Gerald E. "Piaget's Theory." *International Encyclopedia of Psychiatry, Psychology, Psychoanalysis, and Neurology,* s.v. New York: Produced for Aesculapius Publishers by Van Nostrand Reinhold, 1977.

Jacobovitz, Leon A. and Diane Nahl-Jacobvitz. "Learning the Library: Taxonomy of Skills and Errors." *College and Research Libraries* 48 (May 1987): 203-214.

Jacobson, Frances and Michael Jacobson. "Applying Cognitive Theories of Learning to Bibliographic Instruction: A Case Study of End User Searching." Forthcoming. Many of these themes are also discussed by the authors in "Bibliographic Instruction in the Electronic Environment: Incorporating Recent Cognitive Theories of Learning." *Proceedings of the Association of College Research Libraries*, Sixth National Conference, April 1992, Salt Lake City, Utah.

Mager, Robert F. *Preparing Instructional Objectives*. Palo Alto, Calif.: Fearon Publishers, 1962.

McPeck, John E. "Critical Thinking and Subject Specificity: A Reply to Ennis." *Educational Researcher* 19 (May 1990): 11.

Mellon, Constance. "Library Anxiety: A. Grounded Theory and Its Development." *College and Research Libraries* 47 (March 1986): 160-165.

Mellon, Constance. "Information Problem-Solving: A Developmental Approach to Library Instruction." In *Bibliographic Instruction: the Second Generation*, edited by Constance Mellon, 75-89. Littleton, Colo.: Libraries Unlimited, 1987.

Nickerson, Raymond S. "On Improving Thinking Through Instruction." *Review of Research in Education* 15 (1989): 1-57.

Oberman, Cerise. "Avoiding the Cereal Syndrome, or Critical Thinking in the Electronic Environment." *Library Trends* 39, no. 3 (Winter 1991): 189-202.

Paul, Richard W. "Critical Thinking in North America: A New Theory of Knowledge, Learning and Literacy." *Argumentation* 3 (May 1989): 209.

Petrowski, Mary Jane and Lizabeth Wilson. "Avoiding Horror in the Classroom: In-house Training for Bibliographic Instruction." *Illinois Libraries* 73 (February 1991): 180-186.

Rabinoroity, M. and R. Glaser. "Cognitive Structure and Process in Highly Competent Performance." In *The Gifted and Talented: Developmental Perspectives*, edited by F. D. Horowitz and M. O'Brien, Washington, D. C.: American Psychological Association, 1990.

Sandore, Beth A. and Betsy K. Baker. "Attitudes Toward Automation: How They Affect the Services Libraries Provide." In *Proceedings of the American Society for Information Science*, 291-299. Medford, N. J.: Learned Information, 1986.

Spiro, Rand J. , et al. "Knowledge Association for Application: Cognitive Flexibility and Transfer in Complex Content Domains. " In _Executive Control Processes in Reading_, edited by B. K. Britton and S. Glynn, 177-199. Hillsdale, N. J.: Lawrence Erlbaum, 1987.

Spiro, Rand J., et al. "Cognitive Flexibility Theory: Advanced Knowledge Acquisition in Ill-Structured Domains." In _Tenth Annual Conference of the Cognitive Science Society_, 375-383. Hillsdale,N. J.: Lawrence Erlbaum, 1988.

Chapter Two

Instructional Design

Mary Ellen Litzinger
Pennsylvania State University

"What should I do next?" That's the first question most librarians ask themselves when they receive a bibliographic instruction assignment. Many instructors respond to this query by immediately assembling a collection of bibliographies and handouts. While this activity ensures that the instructor will be prepared to teach a class, it ignores a fundamental truth - designing effective bibliographic instruction involves more than simply gathering the right materials. It involves developing objectives that describe what your teaching should accomplish, and using these objectives to plan your lesson and assess its success. Instructional design is a process that provides a framework for accomplishing these tasks. It helps you answer the questions "What should I teach?", "How should I teach?", and "Is my teaching working?". Fundamental to the instructional design process is a belief that instruction is a system of interrelated components or variables (such as the instructor's objectives, a student's prior experience, and available media resources) that contribute collectively to successful learning. For example, a student's prior understanding of Boolean logic can influence both the content of a lesson on keyword searching and the student's ability to successfully search an electronic database. Instructional design provides a framework for gathering information about each system variable and assessing its contribution to the overall success or failure of your instruction.

What is Instructional Design?

Although there are several ways to approach the instructional design process (Reigeluth 1983 and 1987), most instructional design models include these four phases:

Phase 1: Identify the instructional problem ("What do the students need to know?")
Phase 2: Design the solution ("What should I teach?")
Phase 3: Implement the solution ("How should I teach?")
Phase 4: Evaluate the solution ("Was my teaching successful?")

The following diagram illustrates the relationship of these phases:

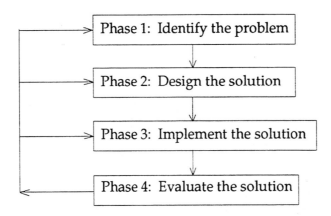

The Instructional Design Process

This diagram suggests that the kind of instructional problem you identify in Phase 1 ("What do the students need to know?") influences the instructional solution that you design in Phase 2 ("What should I teach?") and implement in Phase 3 ("How should I teach?"). The evaluative information developed in Phase 4 ("Was my teaching successful?") helps you revise the content and materials developed in the first three phases. A more complete description of each phase follows.

Phase 1: Identifying the Problem

This phase of the instructional design process answers the question "What do my students need to know?". When you first receive a bibliographic instruction assignment, it is often unclear exactly what students should learn; some BI requests may be as unspecified as "I want my students to find journal articles in the library." It is helpful to consider what skills students should master to accomplish a specific task, such as finding a journal in the library, and to identify the resources available to support this instruction. In conducting this analysis, you should ask yourself this question: "What skills or knowledge do the learners possess now and what skills or knowledge should they possess after instruction?". Needs assessment is a process that provides a framework for structuring this investigation.

A needs assessment compares your goals (i.e., what you want your teaching to accomplish) with existing physical and human resources and determines if these conditions will meet your needs. By knowing which tasks students should accomplish to complete their assignment, identifying the skills they already possess, and listing the human and physical resources available for instruction, you will develop a clearer picture of your instructional problem. This diagram illustrates the relationship of needs assessment to instructional design:

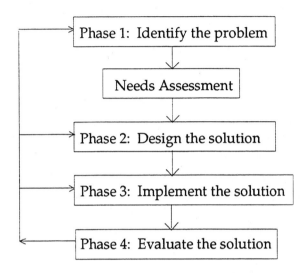

Needs Assessment in the Instructional Design Process

A needs assessment includes four steps:

1. Identifying and ranking desired goals ("What does this class need to know and which of these things are the most important?")

2. Determining existing conditions ("What does this class already know?" "What resources do I have?")

3. Identifying and analyzing discrepancies between desired goals and existing conditions ("What things do I need to teach this class?" "What resources do I need that don't already exist?")

4. Ranking discrepancies ("Which things are the most important to teach this class?" "Which resources are the most necessary for my instruction?") (Pinola 1984)

The following diagram illustrates the relationship among these steps:

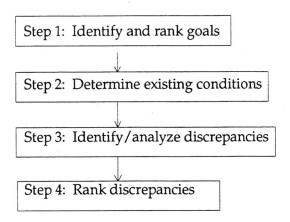

The needs assessment process

A brief discussion of each step follows.

Step 1: Identify and rank desired goals.
There are several ways to determine the goals for a BI class or project, including brainstorming (listing all theoretically possible goals), asking colleagues or administrators for their opinions, consulting teaching faculty, or searching the literature for reports of similar projects. When this list is compiled, you can ask colleagues to rate these goals on a scale (i.e., the most important goal receives ten points, the least important goal receives one point) and compute a mean value for each goal. Use these scores to rank your goals (Pinola 1984).

Step 2: Determine existing conditions.
Using the goals identified in Phase 1, construct a list of skills and resources that would be necessary to meet these goals and determine which of these skills students have already mastered. A common method of compiling this information is to interview library and faculty colleagues and develop a composite picture of your students and their needs. It also may be possible to examine recent examples of student research assignments to determine their relative skill level. Another technique is to question students directly, either orally or through questionnaires. A sample query might be: "Do you agree or disagree with this statement - I feel certain that I can use the online catalog to locate a book in the library?". The information gathered in this phase of the needs assessment can provide the basis for constructing subsequent instructional objectives.

Step 3: Identify and analyze discrepancies between desired goals and existing conditions.
This is the time to compare the goals you identified in Phase 1 with the list of conditions you identified in Phase 2. Very rarely will you find that desired goals exactly match existing conditions, and it is helpful to list these discrepancies in their order of importance.

Step 4: Rank discrepancies.
Using the list of discrepancies you compiled in Phase 3 and keeping in mind the existing conditions you identified in Phase 2, rank the discrepancies you have identified. Ranking can be as simple as compiling lists of "Things that must happen," "Things that would enhance instruction," and "Things I can live without."

Phase 2: Designing the Instructional Solution

This phase of the instructional design process answers the question "What should I teach?". Designing an instructional solution involves: (1) specifying behavioral objectives and (2) developing assessment strategies. This diagram illustrates the relationship of behavioral objectives and assessment strategies to the instructional design process:

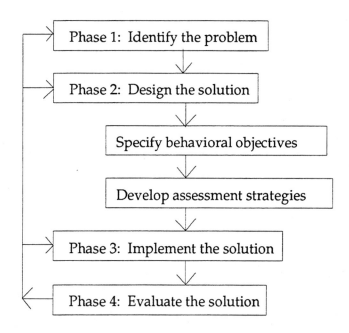

Specifying Behavioral Objectives

Behavioral objectives are a precise statement of the change we can observe in the learner because of instruction. They answer the question "What will learners be able to do after instruction that they could not do before?". Behavioral objectives are the "engine" of the instructional design system, they provide a foundation for designing individual lessons and assessing program success.

What is the best way to write an effective behavioral objective? Although several models are available (Mager 1984), one successful method suggests dividing the objective into five parts:

1. Describe the situation in which the behavior occurs ("What activity will stimulate students to perform what I want to teach them?")
2. Describe the ability that the behavior requires ("What skill(s) does the learner use while performing this activity?")
3. Describe the object of the performance ("What is the outcome/product of the learner's performance?")
4. Describe the action that the learner uses to complete the task ("How will the learner accomplish this activity?")
5. Describe the constraints that govern the performance of the activity ("Should the learner use special tools to perform this activity?" "How well should the learner perform this activity to be considered 'successful'?")

Suppose you are teaching a lesson on using different kinds of information sources. A five part objective for this lesson might read "Given a list of information sources (situation), the learner will classify (ability) the list (object) by identifying primary and secondary sources (action) with ninety percent accuracy (constraint)". The situation portion of the objective describes the stimulus that encourages the learner to perform a behavior. The ability component contains a verb, for example, discriminate, identify, classify, generate, demonstrate, that precisely identifies the ability the learner needs to perform the behavior. The object phrase identifies the outcome or product of the learner's performance. The action verb describes how the performance is to be completed (e.g., by matching, writing, speaking, discussing, pointing, drawing). The constraints phrase identifies the special tools that should be used to perform the activity and defines the level of proficiency that the learner should achieve to be considered "successful" (Gagne and Briggs 1988).

Developing Assessment Strategies

Precisely stated behavioral objectives provide a foundation for constructing tests and other assessment strategies. A good strategy for constructing effective assessment instruments is objective-referenced testing, which suggests that the most effective test questions are those that directly measure the performances that behavioral objectives describe. For example, an objective-referenced question for the objective quoted above would be "Identify the primary and secondary sources included on this list of information sources." Objective-referenced testing encourages you to develop a direct relationship between what you teach and what you test. If this relationship exists, then there is a greater likelihood that your test is valid and measures what you intended. BI assessment strategies can range in complexity from an informal oral question and answer period at the end of class to a more structured test with written essay or multiple choice questions. Some guidelines for developing assessment strategies are:

1.   Include activities that accurately represent your objectives. For example, if your objective specifies that students should classify a list of sources, that activity should be included in your assessment strategy.
2.   Do not aim for a normal distribution of test scores. It is not necessary to have a certain number of "A," "B," and "C" grades in your class to be considered a successful teacher. The purpose of objective- referenced testing is to discover what students have learned, not to confirm that one student's scores are lower or higher than another.
3.   Let your objectives suggest the content of your questions. If your objectives specify that the behavior should be performed using a list, include a list in your question.

Phase 3: Implementing the Instructional Solution

Phases 1 and 2 of the instructional design process help you plan the framework of your instructional project or unit. Once this structure is in place, it is time to consider how you wlll teach the content you have identified. The next section will help you plan an individual lesson.

An effective lesson plan outlines a logical progression of classroom activities that support the learning of the content you identified in Phase 2. Gagne and Briggs, two important pioneers in the instructional design field, maintain that students process classroom information as it is taught, rather than two or three hours later (Gagne, et al. 1988). This information processing occurs internally within each student and is affected by factors such as learning style preferences and learning strategies that develop independently of the instructor. Many psychologists agree that information processing includes these steps:

1.   The learner is stimulated to receive information through one of his senses.
2.   This information is transformed into an image that can be stored in short-term memory.
3.   This image is "coded" into a meaningful phrase and stored in long-term memory.
4.   This phrase is retrieved using cues or search terms from long-term memory and used in the performance of an activity.
5.   The instructor or student provides feedback that reinforces correct performance (E. Gagne 1985).

The instructor can support a student's information processing by:

1.   Gaining the student's attention. This step prepares the student's senses to receive information.
2.   Informing the student of your objectives.
3.   Stimulating the student to recall his or her prior learning. Steps 2 and 3 prepare the student to retrieve previously learned information from long- term memory.

4. Presenting your instructional material. This activity highlights the parts of the lesson that should be saved in short-term memory.

5. Providing guidance as the student processes new information. This step provides the phrases and cues that the student will use to store instructional material in his long-term memory. Steps 4 and 5 represent the teaching portion of the lesson.

6. Providing an opportunity for the student to use new information. This activity allows students to practice retrieving newly learned information.

7. Providing feedback on performance. This step lets the instructor reinforce and refine student learning.

8. Assessing student performance. This step allows students to refine their retrieval cues and receive instructor feedback.

9. Enhancing retention and transfer. This step encourages the student to integrate newly learned information with existing information (Gagne, et al. 1988).

Not all lesson plans will contain each of these steps. You will arrange some of the activities for your students, such as those included in steps 2, 3, and 4, while students may develop some activities themselves. The important thing to remember in lesson planning is that the content and sequence of your classroom activities should support the learning processes of your students.

Phase 4: Evaluating the Instructional Solution

The most critical question in the instructional design process is "Did you meet your instructional goals?". This query is particularly important for newly developed or revised programs. Two processes will help you answer this question: formative evaluation and summative evaluation. This diagram illustrates the relationship of these processes to instructional design:

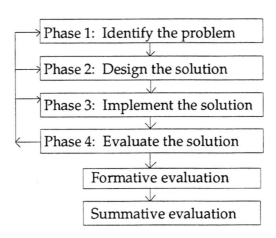

Formative Evaluation

Formative evaluation assesses the effectiveness of your instruction, the objectives, assessment strategies, and lesson plans, and the supporting materials, handouts, booklets, and other media. The goal of formative evaluation is to revise and improve an existing program rather than summarily judge its success or failure. Some methods that can be used to collect formative data are:

1. One-to-one, or clinical testing. The instructor works directly with three or four representative students to identify the most obvious errors in the instruction and obtain initial reactions to its content.
2. Small group evaluation. This process evaluates the effectiveness of the revisions made after the clinical test and determines if students can use the instructional materials without interaction with the instructor. At the conclusion of the evaluation, use a questionnaire to sample student reaction. Some questions that could be included are: Was the instruction interesting? Did you understand what you were supposed to learn? Did you need additional materials to help you understand the instruction? Data obtained from individual student debriefings could supplement the questionnaire results.
3. Field trial. A field trial tests instructional material in an environment that closely resembles the intended instructional situation. For example, if you are evaluating a computer assisted instruction package for basic library users, it might be appropriate to test this package with a group of thirty first year students. Data from the field trial answers these questions:

    - Did I meet the objectives I specified for this unit?
    - Did the instruction have any effects that I didn't anticipate?
    - Can I live with these effects and, if not, what can I change?

Revise your objectives, assessment strategies, lesson plans and instructional material based on the data obtained from each of these processes (Dick and Carey 1985).

Summative Evaluation

At some point after you completed your formative evaluation and implemented a revised version of your instruction, you'll want to answer these questions:

    - Did my students learn what I intended?
    - Did my instruction produce unpredictable side effects?
    - Will my instruction have long-term benefits?

The process of determining the answers to these questions is called summative evaluation and consists of four parts:

1. Analyzing your instructional materials
2. Identifying students' skill levels before instruction
3. Using your instructional materials with a group of students
4. Using a post-test to determine students' skill levels after instruction. You also may administer a questionnaire to measure students' attitude toward the instruction (Dick and Carey 1985).

Other questions that could be asked are:

-What is the comparative cost of this instruction relative to similar programs at my institution?
- Does this instruction have side effects and are they beneficial?
- Does this instruction have long-term benefits?
- When will the instruction be obsolete?
- Has a system been established to ensure its currency?

Chapter Four will provide additional information that you can use to conduct formative and summative evaluation.

Why is Instructional Design Important?

The instructional design process provides a framework for you to identify an instructional problem, and design and implement a solution. The data you generate as part of the instructional design process will help you evaluate the success of your instruction and will target areas for revision. Although the instructional design process may seem complicated at first glance, particularly when applied to a fifty minute BI lecture, the results are worth the effort. It helps you respond more sensitively to the needs of your students while designing and delivering a more effective instructional program. Ultimately, the instructional design process encourages you to become a more thoughtful and accomplished teacher.

References

Dick, Walter and Lou Carey. *The Systematic Design of Instruction*. 2d ed. Glenview, Ill.: Scott Foresman and Co., 1985.

Gagne, Ellen. *The Cognitive Psychology of School Learning*. Boston: Little Brown, 1985.

Gagne, Robert, Leslie Briggs and Walter Wager. *Principles of Instructional Design*. 3d ed. New York: Holt, Rinehart and Winston, 1988.

Mager, Robert. *Preparing Instructional Objectives*. Belmont, Calif.: D. S. Lake, 1984.

Pinola, Mary. "How to Start a Needs Assessment," *Instructional Innovator* 29 (February 1984): 40-45.

Additional References

Anderson, John. *Cognitive Psychology and Its Implications*. New York: W. H. Freeman, 1990.

Briggs, Leslie and Walter W. Wager. *Handbook of Procedures for the Design of Instruction*. 2d ed. Englewood Cliffs, N. J.: Educational Technology Publications, 1981.

Dwyer, Francis M. *Strategies for Improving Visual Learning*. State College, Pa.: Learning Services, 1978.

Gagne, Robert M., ed. *Instructional Technology: Foundations*. Hillsdale, N. J.: Lawrence Erlbaum, 1987.

Gilbert, Thomas F. *Human Competence: Engineering Worthy Performance*. New York: McGraw Hill, 1978.

Mayer, Richard. *Educational Psychology: A Cognitive Approach*, New York: Harper Collins, 1987.

Resier, Robert A. and Gagne, Robert M. *Selecting Media for Instruction*. Englewood Cliffs, N.J.: Educational Technology Publications, 1983.

Spencer, Ken. *The Psychology of Educational Technology and Instructional Media*. London: Routledge, 1988.

Chapter Three

Teaching Methods

Randall Hensley
University of Washington

Many approaches to delivery of instruction content are available to the BI librarian. The decision to use a particular teaching method or combination of methods is not made separate from other decisions regarding instruction, nor is the selection of a teaching method the first aspect of instruction to be determined. This chapter will identify steps for determining a teaching method and will describe major factors that influence the selection of an appropriate method. Finally, definitions of the major teaching method options will be provided along with some considerations relevant to selection and application.

Steps for Determining a Teaching Method

As discussed in Chapters 1 and 2, *defining the goals* the instruction will achieve and *defining the instructional objectives and outcomes* create the context for the teaching method. The goals, objectives, and outcomes are what the teaching method will do.

The process of *describing the audience* for instruction can be as simple as identifying a group as undergraduate or graduate students. It can also be as elaborate as creating a list of what library skills the audience possesses and what educational background the group has. Gender, age, and cultural diversity factors have been shown to be increasingly relevant when determining the method of instruction.

A library skills list in conjunction with *clarifying the appropriate level of instruction* paints a more complete picture of who the audience is and what the audience needs to understand and know how to do. Appropriate level can include such things as information access concepts like "citation", "abstracting service" or "Boolean logic", and such finding skills as "alphabetization", "physical location" or "classification schemes". In arriving at the appropriate level, the librarian also considers the student's understanding of the nature of the discipline and the pattern of its literature. The appropriate level will be much different for a lower division student just beginning to study a discipline than a graduate student. In short, appropriate level is determined by an assessment of what the audience already knows and needs to know in order to successfully complete the assigned task.

Deciding on the appropriate staff for the instruction with regard to skills, qualities, and quantity of staff aims to match the audience with a suitable instructor(s). Previous experience with a similar audience or course content usually produces an advantageous situation both in terms of instructional design, instructor confidence, and credibility with the audience. An instructor's personality, energy level, and knowledge can be matched to instructional goals, objectives, and outcomes. The size of an audience and the level of instruction needed can influence the number of instructors needed.

Determining the materials required to support the instruction results from the goals, objectives, outcomes, audience characteristics, and the level of instruction to be delivered. The knowledge and style of the instructors will also determine the selection of handouts, overheads, media, chalkboards, flipcharts, and the other modes of instruction support available. Even such issues as paper colors, size of print, and the decision to chose a humorous or graphic presentation of information rely on these earlier determinations.

Determining the appropriate facilities for instruction is often the least flexible aspect of the teaching method selection process. However, a choice between library based instruction and regular classroom based instruction is often available, and should be weighed against responses to the previous steps. Chair or table configuration, modification of library workspace, or the use of assignments over some period of time are options to be considered. For example, the librarian may choose to use slides, overheads, and handouts for a presentation because these materials suit the instructional content and the size of the audience. These materials require the use of a facility that has the necessary equipment and seating. The librarian may then choose to use an assignment in order to have the audience practice in the library.

Assessing scheduling requirements for instruction is often a collaborative decision between BI librarian and faculty, and it is more often based upon convenience than an unambiguous commitment to sound instruction. Determining the amount of time necessary for the effective accomplishment of the instruction requires superior negotiation skills and a thorough understanding of what is to be accomplished and why.

Factors That Influence the Selection of a Teaching Method

Certain factors can influence to a greater or lesser degree responses to the steps for determining a teaching method. These factors fall into several categories. Selecting a teaching method that takes these factors into consideration helps insure the success of instruction.

Student readiness for instruction is influenced by how immediate the need for the instruction is. In general, the more immediate the need, the more attention will be given to the instruction by the audience.

Motivation for instruction is determined by a number of elements: people like to learn what interests them; the audience's perception of the relevance of instruction; an individual's desire to succeed not fail; obvious instructor interest in the audience and subject matter; balancing the adult learner's simultaneous desire to and anxiety about working independently and their need for instruction.

Audience *preparation* enhances student readiness for instruction. This preparation can take the form of faculty articulated commitment to library instruction, initial skills inventories, a review of basic skills, or a simple review of expected instructional outcomes. The intent is to prime the audience for learning.

A great deal of research has been done on the relevance of *learning style* as a factor in designing effective instruction. Some teaching methods are more diverse in their ability to appeal to a variety of learning style preferences. One facet of learning styles can be understood as the *information pathways* an audience has available to receive information: visually, orally, through tactile activity, or through individual analysis and organization. Another facet is better understood as analogous to *personality characteristics*: where individuals emphasize such personality attributes as personalization, interpersonal interaction, conceptualization into broader frameworks and analogies, learn-by-doing approaches or analysis of detail, order, and structure. Most individuals have preferred learning styles although most people have learned to operate in a variety of styles. An instructor not mindful of learning style behavior will emphasize their own style when teaching and therefore select a teaching method comfortable for the instructor rather than a considerable percentage of the audience.

The best advice is to select a teaching method that includes a variety of approaches and the ability to modify them during instruction. For example, a workshop might include a period of brief lecture, audience participation, slides, and note taking. Most BI instruction is with *adult learners* and adult learners generally appreciate three elements in instruction: solving problems, sharing knowledge, and making applications. A teaching method that incorporates these approaches holds the promise of greater success.

An emergent consideration is that of *diversity*. Ethnic, cultural, gender, and age factors influence learning. What is less clear is how best to incorporate these factors into the design of instruction. Research points to differences in the effectiveness of teaching methods that emphasize verbal, affective, visual, and interactive approaches. Some learning style theory has examined the relationship between diversity categories and field dependence/field independence. Teaching methods that can accommodate greater interaction between teacher and student and that can incorporate a variety of approaches to content are showing initial success in reaching diverse populations.

Another factor to be considered when selecting a teaching method is the *instructor's ability to utilize a teaching method*. While this factor might strike some as obvious it is important for a BI librarian to realize that they may not be able to effectively deliver instruction by means of a particular teaching method. This inability may be due to the instructor's own strong learning style preference, a lack of familiarity with a particular method, or an absence of effective modeling for the method to be used. Most instructional situations are suitable to more than one teaching method. Building a repertoire of methods with which an instructor is comfortable offers assurance of effective instruction.

Time available to devote to instruction influences teaching method selection. Time released by faculty for library instruction, staff time available for instruction, student time available to receive and practice content, instructor preparation time, and actual instruction delivery time, all must be taken into consideration. In fact, *student practice* constitutes a major factor in itself. Learning without practice is learned helplessness. Not every teaching method manifests practice time but the need for an audience to put into effect the content of instruction must be accounted for in the method selection. This practice can occur individually with the support of reference desk staff that has been made aware of student tasks and the instruction received. Practice is an integral aspect of some methods. The question does need to be asked: "where's the practice?" as part of the method selection process.

Finally, *available facilities and equipment,* and *costs* influence the choice of teaching method. Are the facilities I need for a particular teaching method actually available? Can I modify the existing facilities to suit the needs of the method? Is the equipment I need available? Is it operational and can unexpected situations be handled? While it may not always be necessary to determine the absolute costs of a particular method in order to select it, it is important for the BI librarian to understand what costs are involved. This understanding helps make the selection process realistic and ultimately justifiable.

Teaching Method Options: Definitions and Considerations

Each of the following teaching methods are explained by providing: a definition, a list of factors to be considered when selecting the method, and an example of an application of the method. Items from the bibliography at the end of this chapter that are particularly relevant to the method are indicated with the author's last name in parentheses.

Course-related Instruction
> Definition
>> Broad category of instruction that provides information about sources and strategies for a specific course or assignment; usually one class period.

> Considerations
>> - duration of instruction common to most academic settings
>> - student readiness for instruction usually high
>> - wide variety of models available in the BI literature
>> - library instruction supports course goals
>> - standardization of content and instruction materials possible
>> - content can be modified for different audiences and levels of instruction
>> - can be applied to large segments of a curriculum
>> - provides personal contact between audience and BI librarian
>> - duration of instruction not conducive to extensive in-class practice nor extensive application of learning style variety
>> - can be suitable for adult learners
>> - requests for instruction usually required by a number of courses during same periods of the academic calendar
>> - requires substantial commitment of staff

> Common application
>> Faculty requests instruction for a course in a particular discipline; students have been assigned a paper that requires gathering information on a topic; the instruction will occur during regular class time which lasts fifty minutes; class size is approximately twenty-five students (Beaubien 1982; Oberman 1982; Roberts 1989).

Course-integrated Instruction

Definition

Broad category of instruction that provides information about sources and strategies is integrated into the course objectives as essential course content; usually multiple class periods and often in a variety of formats, including lecture, learning activity, group work; course design is usually a collaboration between BI librarian and faculty.

Considerations

- merging of course and library instruction goals, objectives, and outcomes
- opportunity for a variety of content, activity, and assignment
- student readiness for instruction is high and can be maintained
- wide variety of models available in the BI literature
- opportunity for modification of content and approach during the course
- provides personal contact between audience and BI librarian and opportunity for high credibility with audience
- duration of instruction can be conducive to extensive in-class practice and extensive application of learning style variety
- well suited to adult learners
- requires well developed faculty relationships
- requires substantial commitment of staff and instruction design time
- may require discipline or subject expertise for the BI librarian
- can impact a relatively smaller number of students than course-related instruction

Common application

Faculty and BI librarian design a course for a particular discipline that incorporates gathering and interpreting information throughout the duration of the course; students will be assigned a number of projects; the BI librarian will teach a variety of skills and topics; the instruction will occur a number of times during regular class time; class size is approximately twenty-five students (Kohn 1986; Roberts 1989).

Lecture

Definition

A speech providing information about sources and strategies; noted for the one directional nature of the communication with limited ability for audience interaction.

Considerations

- mode of instruction is common to an academic setting
- duration of instruction is common to an academic setting and the length can be easily modified
- student readiness for instruction can be sufficient but motivation factor can be low
- wide variety of models available in the BI literature
- can be designed for application to different situations such as different physical sites and configurations, and classroom sizes

- a large amount of information can be transmitted at one time
- provides some personal contact
- allows for minimal application of learning style variety
- minimally suited to adult learners
- can maintain utility over time with minimal revision
- can impact large numbers of students

Common application

Faculty requests that the BI librarian instruct a large lecture course for a particular discipline about how to find information for a particular project; instruction will occur in the regular classroom which is a large lecture hall; class size is approximately one hundred fifty students (Breivik 1982; Roberts 1989).

Active Learning
Definition

Instruction where the responsibility for learning is shared by instructor and students; a variety of activities comprise the instruction so that students actively participate in the identification of instruction content and its application to their needs; experiential learning, student-centered learning, cooperative learning, and collaborative learning are generally analogous.

Considerations
- mode of instruction is gaining credibility at alternative and small colleges and community colleges
- duration of instruction is flexible but usually requires more time than lecture approach because of reliance on activity and discussion
- student readiness for instruction is high
- models exist more often in the education and community college literature
- high flexibility for application to different situations
- smaller amount of information can be transmitted at any given time but retention value is considered to be high
- provides high quality personal contact
- allows for extensive application of learning style variety
- highly suited to adult learners
- staff time intensive
- requires high level of teaching skills
- can impact large number of students programmatically but not large groups in a single instructional setting

Common application
  Faculty requests that the BI librarian facilitate the discovery of library based
  techniques for understanding the background of a particular author; students are
  divided into three task groups with specific assignments; task groups are given time
  to work on assignments; BI librarian facilitates discussion of task groups work; class
  is held in the library during class time; class size is approximately twenty-five
  students (Moran 1990).

Orientation
  Definition
    Designed to introduce an audience to the services, facilities, and physical organiza-
    tion of a library.

  Considerations
    - mode of instruction is common to all library settings
    - duration of session is extremely flexible
    - student readiness for instruction may be low if audience requires information about
      sources and strategies along with orientation
    - wide variety of models available in the BI literature
    - flexibility for media and printed materials applications and for delivery by different
      levels of staff
    - limited amount of information can be transmitted
    - provides personal contact which may be useful in alleviating audience frustration
      and anxiety about library physical organization
    - allows for minimal application of learning style variety
    - minimally suited to adult learners depending on the capabilities of the format such
      as type of media selected, duration of the orientation and comfort level of audience
      to ask questions
    - staff time intensive if delivered by individuals or in design and revision of media
      and printed materials versions
    - requires some expertise and training to perform effectively
    - audience size dependent on physical configuration of library

  Common application
    BI librarian provides a tour of the library to approximately fifteen students; explains
    the function of the reference desk, circulation and reserve desks, books, periodicals,
    indexes, CD-ROM products, and online catalog while taking the students to the
    location of each (Breivik 1982; Roberts 1989).

Courses

Definition

Instruction that is a formal offering of a curriculum in the standard form and duration of an institution's courses; students usually receive credit in accordance with institutional regulations.

Considerations

- mode of instruction is common to academic settings
- duration of instruction usually dictated by institutional practice
- student readiness for instruction can be high
- wide variety of models available in the BI literature
- flexibility for applications to different situations depending on instructor expertise in instructional design
- high flexibility in the amount of information that can be transmitted
- provides high level of personal contact and opportunities for faculty relations
- allows for maximum application of learning style variety
- highly suited to adult learners
- staff time intensive in both delivery of instruction and course design
- requires teaching expertise
- audience size limited

Common application

BI librarian teaches a semester long course for a particular academic department about the organization of information and information resources for that department's discipline; students receive two units of credit and are graded on tests and written assignments; course is comprised of a mixture of lecture, orientation to the library, assignments, discussion, and active learning experiences; course meets twice a week for fifty minutes; class size is approximately thirty students (Pastine 1989; Roberts 1989).

Point-Of-Use

Definition

Instruction at the site of a particular resource or service; forms include printed materials, media, signage, and computerized programs.

Considerations

- mode of instruction is common to all library settings
- duration of instruction is most effective when limited to essential information
- student readiness for instruction can be high depending on the match with student need
- wide variety of models available in the BI literature
- flexibility for applications to different situations depending on production capabilities and staff time for design and revision

- audience reliance on scanning and emphasis on problem solving limits amount of information that can be transmitted
- no personal contact
- limited application of learning style variety
- minimally suited to adult learners
- moderately staff time intensive in terms of design and revision
- requires production expertise depending on form
- audience size large

Common application

Explanation sheet for using a CD-ROM product attached to the workstation; signage detailing how to use the library's periodical list; media program in the index area explaining how to use periodical indexes generally (Kupersmith 1980; Roberts 1989).

Printed Guides

Definition

Instruction in the form of printed materials that can identify resources, communicate strategy, and explain the structure of a source; common forms are bibliographies, subject guides, pathfinders, and instructional handouts.

Considerations

- mode of instruction is common to all library settings
- duration of instruction is usually most effective when limited to essential information
- student readiness for instruction can be high depending on the match with student need
- wide variety of models available in the BI literature
- high flexibility for applications to different situations depending on production capabilities and staff time for design and revision
- audience reliance on scanning and emphasis on problem solving limits amount of information that can be transmitted
- no personal contact but can be used to enhance and support personal contacts
- limited application of learning style variety
- minimally suited to adult learners
- moderately staff time intensive in terms of design and revision
- audience size large

Common application

Explanation brochure about how to use the library; subject guides listing reference books for different subjects; flow chart handout about how to find periodicals in the library (Jackson 1984; Roberts 1989).

Workbooks

Definition

Instruction in the form of an organized series of printed explanations and practice designed to cover the basic issues of library location, information resources, and search strategy.

Considerations

- mode of instruction is common in academic library settings
- duration of instruction can be variable depending on how the instruction is incorporated into the curriculum, how the instruction is assigned to students, and how long the explanations and practice are
- student readiness for instruction can be moderate depending on the match with student need
- wide variety of models available in the BI literature
- moderate flexibility for applications to different situations depending on production capabilities and staff time for modification
- high flexibility in the amount of information that can be transmitted
- some personal contact depending on the direction given to the audience for completion, but requires high degree of personal involvement of the audience and usually provides regular feedback
- moderate application of learning style variety
- suitable to adult learners
- moderately staff time intensive in terms of initial design and revision
- audience size large

Common application

All undergraduate students must complete a library use workbook as part of their work in a required English course; the thirty page workbook has sections about the physical location of materials, the use of the online catalog, use of indexes, the library's classification system, and formulating a successful search strategy; each section provides brief information followed by an exercise; exercises are regularly graded by the library staff; students complete the workbook during a two-week period; class size is approximately two hundred students (Oberman 1982; Phipps 1980).

Videotape

Definition

Instruction using visual images and audio content, produced or transmitted by a television system and stored on tape.

Considerations

- mode of instruction is common in many library settings
- duration of instruction can be variable but is usually limited to not more than sixty minutes

- student readiness for instruction can be high as long as production quality is high
- a variety of models available in the BI literature
- flexibility for applications to different situations must be incorporated into the initial production because modification is time consuming and often costly
- moderate flexibility in the amount of information that can be transmitted
- personal contact depending on how the instruction is used but instruction can incorporate high affect and a personal approach
- low application of learning style variety
- some suitability to adult learners
- very staff time intensive in terms of initial design and revision but minimal staff time involved in subsequent use; require access to productions skills and facilities
- audience size large

Common application

A videotaped tour of the library showing locations and including short interviews with staff and users; a videotaped explanation of a search strategy with a mixture of location and resource visuals, close-ups of key elements, and narrative visuals of major points (Breivik 1982; MacDonald 1991; Roberts 1989).

Audiotape

Definition

Instruction using recorded sound content stored on tape.

Considerations

- mode of instruction is common in many library settings
- duration of instruction can be variable but is usually limited to not more than thirty minutes
- student readiness for instruction can be high depending on production quality and application of the form
- a variety of models available in the BI literature
- limited flexibility for applications to different situations because of audience desire for visuals to accompany audio
- moderate flexibility in the amount of information that can be transmitted
- minimal personal contact depending on how the instruction is used; minimal ability to incorporate a personal approach
- low application of learning style variety
- some suitability to adult learners
- staff time intensive in terms of initial design and revision but minimal staff time involved in subsequent use; requires access to production skills and facilities
- audience size moderate

Common application
>   An audiotape tour of the library showing locations and explaining services (Breivik).

Slide/tape
Definition
>   Instruction using a set of visual slides and explanatory audiotape.

Considerations
>   - mode of instruction is common in many library settings
>   - duration of instruction can be variable but is usually limited to not more than thirty minutes
>   - student readiness for instruction can be high depending on production quality and application of the form
>   - a variety of models available in the BI literature
>   - flexibility for applications to different situations should be incorporated into the initial production but modifications are less time consuming and costly than those for videotape
>   - moderate flexibility in the amount of information that can be transmitted
>   - personal contact depending on how the instruction is used but instruction can incorporate affect and a personal approach
>   - low application of learning style variety
>   - some suitability to adult learners
>   - staff time intensive in terms of initial design and revision but minimal staff time involved in subsequent use; requires access to production skills and facilities
>   - audience size large

Common application
>   Slide/tape tour of the library showing locations and an explanation of services; a slide/tape explanation of a search strategy with a mixture of location and resource visuals, close-ups of key elements, narrative visuals of major points and audio narration (Breivik 1982; Crow 1989; Roberts 1989).

Computer-assisted Instruction
Definition
>   Instruction designed with a program operating on a computer; usually supplies information, poses questions, and provides responses.

Considerations
>   - mode of instruction is available in some academic library settings
>   - duration of instruction can be variable
>   - student readiness for instruction can be high depending on the match with student need and because computer technology is attractive
>   - models available in the BI literature

- flexibility for applications to different situations depending on design capabilities, staff time for modification, and availability of computer hardware
- high flexibility in the amount of information that can be transmitted
- interaction with computer can substitute for satisfaction derived from personal contact
- moderate application of learning style variety
- suitable to adult learners
- very staff time intensive in terms of initial design but low in terms of revision
- audience size dependent on availability of computer hardware
- can incorporate immediate feedback to audience about success or failure

Common application

A microcomputer program that introduces students to physical location of library services and materials, basic information about reference books, online catalog, and periodical indexes; program uses hypertext capability and is used on library dedicated microcomputer workstations (Bourne 1990; Chaffin 1987; MacDonald 1991).

Interactive Multimedia

Definition

Instruction designed with a program operating on a computer that combines visual images, moving or still, and sound with other aspects of computer technology; instruction usually supplies information, poses questions, and provides responses.

Considerations

- mode of instruction is beginning to be available in some library settings
- duration of instruction can be variable
- student readiness for instruction can be high depending on the match with student need and because this type of enhanced computer technology offers greater variety in the transmission of information
- some models available in the BI literature; models available in the computer and instructional technology literature
- high flexibility in the amount of information that can be transmitted
- interaction with computer and multimedia approach to information transmission can substitute for satisfaction derived from personal contact
- flexibility for applications to different situations depending on design capabilities, staff time for design and modification, and availability of interactive software and hardware, and the availability of computer hardware
- moderate application of learning style variety; potentially better than computer assisted instruction
- suitable to adult learners
- very staff time intensive in terms of initial design and moderate in terms of revision
- audience size dependent on availability of computer hardware
- can incorporate immediate feedback to audience about success or failure

Common application
    An interactive multimedia, computer assisted program that explains the services
    and collections of a library through use of voice narration, video and slide generated
    images, graphics and text (Kautz 1988).

The Issue of Practice

Earlier in this chapter, under "Factors That Influence the Selection of a Teaching Method," the
issue of *student practice* as the need for an audience to put into effect the content of instruction
was presented. There are a variety of practice "exercise" examples available in the BI literature.
Practice exercises can be considered within two broad categories.

Exercises as Part of Instruction
    1. Oral reiteration of key points by students
    2. BI librarian generated questions to students
    3. Individual or group applications of instruction
    4. Student driven question and answer periods
    5. Workbooks that include assignments
    6. Computer assisted instruction with questions included in instruction design
    7. Active learning where students demonstrate or supply information
    8. Interactive multimedia with questions included in instruction design

Exercises as Assignments after Instruction
    1. Analysis of faculty assigned student project that instruction was intended to
       facilitate
    2. Assignments where students demonstrate an understanding of the instruction
    3. Tests where students verify retention of the instruction

This need to practice must be incorporated into the teaching method selection process in order
to maximize the effectiveness of the method.

Knowledge of teaching methods must incorporate an understanding of the steps to take when
selecting a method. That knowledge includes an understanding of the factors influencing the
selection of a particular method. The application of this knowledge is the design and delivery
of instruction that actually teaches.

References

Beaubien, Anne K., Sharon A. Hogan, and Mary W. George. *Learning the Library: Concepts and Methods For Effective Bibliographic Instruction.* New York: Bowker, 1982.

Bodi, Sonia. "Teaching Effectiveness and Bibliographic Instruction: the Relevance of Learning Styles." *College and Research Libraries* 51 (1990): 113-119.

Bourne, Donna E. "Computer Assisted Instruction, Learning Theory, and Hypermedia: An Associative Linkage." *Research Strategies* 8 (1990): 160-171.

Breivik, Patricia. *Planning the Library Instruction Program.* Chicago: American Library Association, 1982.

Chaffin, J. "Macintosh-Assisted Library Orientation Tour." *College and Research Libraries News* 6 (June 1987): 332-334.

Crow, Kathryn Moore. "Effective Use of Slides For Bibliographic Instruction." *Research Strategies* 7 (1989): 175-179.

Hall, Patrick Andrew. "The Role and Affectivity in Instructing People of Color: Some Implications for Bibliographic Instruction." *Library Trends* 39, no. 3 (1991): 316-326.

Jackson, William J. "The User Friendly Library Guide." *College and Research Libraries News* 9 (October 1984): 468-473.

Jones, Dionne J. "Cognitive Styles: Sex and Ethnic Differences." Paper presented at the Annual Meeting of the American Educational Research Association, Washington, D.C., November 13-15, 1986. ERIC Document # 284 907.

Kautz, Barbara A., Patricia M. Rodkewich, Will D. Philipson, and Jane Bardon. "Evaluation of a New Library Instruction Concept: Interactive Video." *Research Strategies* 6 (1988): 109-117.

Kohn, David and Lizabeth A. Wilson. "Effectiveness of Course-Integrated Bibliographic Instruction in Improving Coursework." *RQ* 26 (1986): 206-211.

Kupersmith, John. "Information Graphics and Sign Systems as Library Instruction Media." *Drexel Library Quarterly* 16 (1980): 56-68.

MacDonald, Linda Brew, Mara R. Saule, Margaret W. Gordon, Craig A. Robertson. *Teaching Technologies in Libraries: A Practical Guide.* Boston: G.K. Hall, 1991.

Moran, B.B. "Library/Classroom Partnerships For the 1990's: Increasing Active Learning in Undergraduate Education." *College and Research Libraries News* 51 (1990): 511-514.

Oberman, Cerise and Katina Strauch. *Theories of Bibliographic Education: Designs For Teaching.* New York: Bowker, 1982.

Pastine, Maureen and Bill Katz. *Integrating Library Use Skills into the General Education Curriculum.* New York: Haworth Press, 1989.

Phipps, Shelley E. "Why Use Workbooks? Or Why Do Chickens Cross the Road? And Other Metaphors, Mixed." *Drexel Library Quarterly* 16 (1980): 41-53.

Ramirez, Manuel. "Cognitive Styles and Cultural Diversity." Paper presented at the Annual Meeting of the American Educational Research Association, New York, NY, March 19-23, 1982. ERIC Document # 218 380.

Roberts, Anne F. and Susan G. Blandy. *Library Instruction For Librarians.* 2d rev. ed. Englewood, Colo.: Libraries Unlimited, 1989.

Sheridan, Jean. "The Reflective Librarian: Some Observations on Bibliographic Instruction in the Academic Library." *Journal of Academic Librarianship* 16 (1990): 22-26.

Chapter Four

Evaluation

Mignon S. Adams
Philadelphia College of Pharmacy and Science

"Evaluation" is a term that evokes unpleasant feelings in many of us. The root of the word "evaluate" means to "set a value on," and few of us want to be in a situation in which we are going to be judged and found wanting. Who looks forward to an annual personnel evaluation? Perhaps this negative connotation is the reason that so many otherwise excellent bibliographic instruction librarians, who plan their teaching well, fail to follow through. They do not collect the information they need to improve their teaching or to document the very good job they're doing.

Why Evaluate?

Evaluation, as the term is used in education, means the systematic gathering of information in order to make decisions. The information gathered can be used to make decisions of high importance to bibliographic instruction librarians, decisions such as these:

Decision: How Can Teaching Be Improved? Every teacher needs feedback on whether or not the content of a lesson was appropriate, or if presentation skills can be improved, or if important concepts were explained in an understandable way.

Decision: Am I Doing OK? Many librarians have not been trained as teachers. A coordinator of BI can use evaluation techniques to provide positive feedback to support and encourage the efforts of fledgling instructors.

Decision: Retention, Promotion and Tenure. Librarians being considered for personnel decisions have a much stronger case if they have documentation of the job they're doing. Reports of the number of classes taught or the students served are not nearly so effective as survey responses or test results.

Decision: Is This Program Worth It? In times of financial exigency, any program which consumes time and resources needs to be justified. Don't wait until budget cuts are announced; have information ready which proves that a program is accomplishing worthy objectives.

All of these decisions are ones that every instruction librarian is faced with. Far from being a negative experience, evaluation can be a tool to demonstrate the effectiveness of a program and the expertise of the people conducting it.

Approaches to Evaluation

Practitioners in many different disciplines use evaluation, and their approaches are somewhat different. *Educators* use evaluation to measure student achievement in order to assign grades, to place students properly, or to ascertain teacher effectiveness. Their instruments of most concern are tests, both teacher-made and standardized.

In higher education, evaluation of colleges is carried out by both regional and professional accrediting agencies. There does not appear to be a common theoretical basis for these evaluations, but agencies tend to operate in similar manners. Within the last decade, their interest has changed from "input measures," such as faculty qualifications, number of books in the library etc., to an emphasis on "outcome measures."

The need to evaluate publicly-funded social programs gave rise to what some consider the profession of *program evaluators*. Techniques developed by these evaluators are designed to look at the impact of total programs, whether they have been implemented correctly and whether they meet their objectives.

Sociologists and *market researchers* are interested in discerning opinions. They have developed sophisticated techniques for surveying what people actually think and believe.

Bibliographic instruction librarians can use the techniques of all these groups. Because they teach, BI practitioners should learn how to construct tests which actually measure what students have learned. BI librarians are also in charge of programs with many different parts, so they can profit from the work that program evaluators have done. Because those in BI deal with consumers (and both students and participating classroom faculty can be considered as consumers), student opinions can also be important. Instruction librarians may at various times be interested in the techniques of each of the groups named above. The sources listed at the end of this chapter serve as a guide to their respective literatures.

When beginning to think about evaluation, instruction librarians need to be familiar with some of the basic concepts referred to by evaluators. The terms described in the following section are used in more than one discipline.

Evaluation Concepts

Needs Assessment   If you don't know where you are at the beginning, you don't know where you're going or what you need to get there. A needs assessment is an evaluation of the present state of affairs, in order to determine whether improvement is necessary and what kind of program, if any, can make an improvement.

In a needs assessment, the evaluator surveys the opinions of people in a position to know what the needs are - faculty, graduating students, alumni, administrators, for example. Materials such as test results or student papers may also serve as documentation. Once all this information is gathered and analyzed, then appropriate decisions can be made about the desirability, shape and content of the proposed program.

Most bibliographic instruction programs are undertaken without a formal needs assessment. Some just grow gradually, from a few classes to many. Others are based on the assumptions of those in charge of the program, and these assumptions may or may not be correct. Even though a program was begun without a formal needs assessment, such an assessment can be done at any time, with the purpose of clarifying goals or identifying unmet ones. Questions answered by this kind of evaluation include: What should we be doing? Are we neglecting important areas? What parts of the program should have the highest priorities?

Formative Evaluation   On a regular, ongoing basis, instruction librarians need information so that they know which parts of their teaching are done well, and which should be done better. Gathering this kind of information is called "formative evaluation," because it can result in improvements and modifications in teaching.

Techniques of formative evaluation can include surveys asked of students immediately after instruction, post-tests, or examinations of student projects. The information gained answers to such questions as: What is the best method of teaching X? Were my presentation skills adequate? Was the right content covered in this lecture?

Summative Evaluation   Should a program be continued? This is the basic question which a summative evaluation is designed to answer. While the daily activities of a BI program can be carried on without a summative evaluation, in times of financial exigency it is entirely possible that coordinators of programs may suddenly be asked to justify the time and expense devoted to them. If data has been collected, the BI librarian has the information to describe what the program is designed to achieve and documentation to demonstrate that it is meeting its goals.

Outcomes Assessment   Outcomes assessment is a currently popular term in higher education, one recently adopted by state legislators and accrediting agencies. Simply put, "outcomes assessment" means to look not at efforts and expenditures, but their results: to measure changes in performance and behavior. For example, libraries have traditionally been evaluated by the size of their holdings or the number of hours they are open ("input measures"). An outcomes assessment might look at the number of users served, or whether the users perceive that they have access to what they need. In BI, an outcomes assessment would not be concerned with the number of instructional sessions or the qualifications of the instructor, but rather would consider if students have become better library users as the result of instruction. Questions answered by an outcomes assessment include: How are students different after the instruction program? Has satisfaction with the library increased? All the approaches described in this section could provide evidence which could be used in an outcomes assessment.

Qualitative Evaluation   Most of the techniques discussed in this chapter refer to goal based designs of teaching and evaluation, designs which grew out of the need in both world wars to train large numbers of recruits in various skills. However, by the seventies, many evaluators had grown dissatisfied by what they deemed an over-reliance on "quantitative evaluation," an approach they considered to be too concerned about numbers and objective data. They looked instead at methods developed by sociologists and anthropologists which they felt gave them understanding and insight into the people and programs they were studying.

Qualitative evaluators believe that numbers cannot yield richness and depth of knowledge. They feel that undertaking an evaluation which seeks to measure the achievement of pre-determined goals precludes the opportunity to discover that a program might be meeting altogether unexpected, perhaps even more desirable, ones. While many quantitative program evaluators have begun to include qualitative techniques in their work, an adherence to one or the other approach still divides evaluators into two distinct groups.

Techniques used in qualitative evaluation include in-depth interviews, direct observation, case studies, and analysis of written materials such as diaries, correspondence, or open-ended responses on questionnaires. Questions which might be answered include: How do students use libraries? How do students really feel about our program? Is the program achieving what was planned for it, or does it actually accomplish something else? For example, rather than teaching students to be proficient library users, we may be teaching them that library research is frustrating drudgery.

Depending on what information is sought, BI librarians can avail themselves of many different techniques, using the approach of whatever discipline might be helpful. The rest of this chapter is concerned with the consideration of various questions instruction librarians may want to ask, and which may be answered by one approach or another of varying disciplines.

What Do You Want To Know?

The reason for doing any evaluation is to gather information in order to make decisions. Therefore, the most important step is to determine what you want to know. At the beginning of this chapter, some important decisions for instruction librarians were listed, such as how can teaching be improved? or is this program doing what it should?

Many different instruments can be used to answer these questions. Following is a list of questions, which you may be interested in answering for yourself or your institution, matched with instruments which, appropriately designed, could provide the answers.

To Answer These Questions   **Use These Instruments**

Were presentation skills adequate?   - Student survey, immediately after
                                                    presentation
                                                - Checklist filled out by observing peer
                                                - Videotape viewed afterward with checklist

What is the right level to present the materials?	- Pre-test of students to determine what they already know
Was the content appropriate?	- Student survey after their assignments/projects are completed
Did students learn from the presentation?	- Post-test on materials - Survey of student opinion (NOTE: this will yield only whether students <u>think</u> they learned-not what they actually did.)
Could students apply what was taught to them?	- Worksheet which asks them to apply context of presentation - Examination of assignment/project - Assignments which ask students to do what was taught - Post-test which asks application questions - Student journal, kept throughout research process - Observation of student library use
What skills do faculty think students should have?	- Faculty survey - Interviews with faculty
What is the best way to teach a concept?	- Post-test or survey after each
Is the program making a difference?	- Test of both freshmen and seniors - Examination of assignments/projects - Test of randomly-selected seniors - Survey of graduates currently in graduate school or working
Do students feel more comfortable in the library as a result of the BI program?	- Attitude scale - Interviews

Note that some of the questions concern the improvement of teaching (formative evaluation), some on selecting appropriate goals (needs assessment), and some on assessing the total impact of the program (summative evaluation). One instrument cannot serve all these purposes. Feedback to improve your teaching skills requires a different approach from assessing your total program.

Developing Instruments

All of us want to be the very best teachers we can be. Receiving feedback from our students or our peers can help us. While various instruments can be used to get systematic feedback, the same basic method is used to develop any instrument.

Steps in Developing an Evaluation Instrument

1. Decide what general questions you want answered and choose an appropriate type of instrument (see previous chart).
2. Make a list of the specific questions you want answered. For example, if you are interested in presentation skills, your list might include questions on eye contact, movement, questioning techniques; if you want to determine what students already know, you may want to know whether they understand Boolean logic or have used a periodical index before.
3. Share this list with others who may be concerned, such as other librarians in the instruction program. They may have valuable suggestions.
4. Write the items for the measure in rough draft form.
5. Pilot the measure by having someone else read and react to the items. Use someone from the target population, for instance a student worker, to react to clarity and wording. Other librarians will know what your jargon means, so they are not the best reactors.
6. Don't explain why your reader should have understood the item correctly; revise it. Your goal is to write the best items you can, not to prove yourself right.

An instruction librarian can develop any of the following measures by using the steps outlined above.

Types of Instruments

Pre-Test
Typical Uses:
- to determine what students already know, so that content of a presentation is on the correct level
- to create a benchmark for comparison with a later post-test to demonstrate what students have learned
- to demonstrate to students that they do not already know everything about the library

Considerations:
- should be objective for quick grading
- if it is to be given in a class meeting before coming to the library, it should be brief

- if it is to be used to establish what students already know, questions asking students to define or identify terms may be used
- if it is to be used to accompany a post-test, questions should call for application and evaluation. For example, a student could be asked to identify *Social Sciences Index* as a periodicals index, but asked to apply that knowledge by selecting an index which would lead to an article in a professional psychology journal

Sources of Help:
- any basic educational measurement text (Ebel and Frisbie 1986)
- education faculty
- computer center, for using machine-scored answer sheets and standard statistical packages

Post-Test

Typical Uses:
- immediately after instruction to determine if students understood; and to reinforce learning
- after students' completion of projects/assignments to see if they retained instruction
- to compare with a pre-test in order to document how much student learning occurred

Considerations:
- although most of the test should be objective for quick scoring, at least one open-ended question should be included in order to gain insight into students' reactions
- questions which call only for identification and definition should be avoided; instead, most questions should ask for application and evaluation

Sources of Help:
- same as for pre-test

Performance Measures

Typical Uses:
- to demonstrate that students can apply what they've learned
- to increase the opportunity for student practice

Considerations:
- worksheets administered directly after instruction can provide both an opportunity for practice as well as simulation of a real activity
- when students complete projects or research papers they are applying what they have learned
- paper-and-pencil tests can be a performance measure if students are given situations to respond to
- observation of students' behavior can be a performance measure
- the term "performance measure" is often used interchangeably with "out comes assessment"

Sources of Help:
- education faculty on your campus
- examples of performance measures (Morris 1987)

Surveys

Typical Uses:
- to solicit student opinion on presentation skills
- to solicit student opinion on the instructional session after their assignments/ projects are completed
- to gather faculty opinion on the goals of the BI program
- to gather information from graduates on the program

Considerations:
- wording is critical in a survey; no survey item should ever be used without piloting
- pertinent demographic information may be helpful in interpreting survey results
- leave space for comments and at least one open-ended response

Sources of Help:
- any basic survey research text (Payne 1981)
- sociologists or market researchers on your campus

Checklists

Typical uses:
- to guide peer observation of presentation skills
- to guide a self-reviewed video to observe presentation skills
- to guide observation of student behavior to determine how a library is used after instruction

Considerations:
- the checklist should consist of specific, observable behaviors in order to avoid subjective decisions
- those concerned should agree upon the behaviors' meanings, e.g., that the behaviors listed constitute good presentation skills, or appropriate library use
- space should be left to write in examples

Sources of Help:
- basic works on the behavior being studied, e.g., speechmaking; see Appendix B
- communications faculty on your campus

Attitude Scales

Typical Uses:
- to ascertain students' feelings toward the instructional session
- to measure changes in attitudes before and after instruction

Considerations:
- much research has been conducted on the construction and effectiveness of attitude scales; two standard ones are the Likert scale and the Osgood semantic differential scale

- the Likert scale - five opinions from "strongly agree" to "strongly disagree" is often used on opinion surveys
- again, wording is critical

Sources of Help:
- basic texts on attitude surveys (Schuman 1981)
- sociologists or marketing researchers on your campus

Interviews

Typical Uses:
- to determine others' perspectives on the goals of the program
- to uncover in-depth student feelings

Considerations:
- properly done, interviews can yield rich insights into people's feelings and motivation
- interviews are time-consuming; if all that is needed is factual data collection, then a survey is preferable
- "focus groups" are group interviews and as such can decrease time spent interviewing (focus groups have other attributes as well)
- good interviewing is an art, and should be prepared for and practiced
- depending on the purpose of the interview, it may be open-ended and unstructured, planned along guidelines, or consist of completely prepared questions

Source of Help:
- market researchers or psychologists on your campus
- works on interviewing

Program Evaluation

All of the instruments described in the previous section can be used to discover strengths and weaknesses of various parts of a BI program. However, at times it may be desirable to look at the program *in toto,* in order to answer the questions: Is this program effective? Is it doing what it should?

Reasons For a Program Evaluation
- A new BI coordinator may want to examine the program to identify its strengths and weaknesses
- A change in library administration may lead to questioning the BI program's effectiveness
- A mandate from college administrators or accrediting agency may call for assessing outcomes
- Due to financial exigency, the college or library administration may demand justification for all programs

- Staff cutbacks may force a reallocation of staff
- The BI Coordinator may wish to make a case for increased funding or staff

A whole profession of program evaluation has emerged, in response to the need to measure the effectiveness of publicly-funded social programs. One response to the need of a program evaluation might be to have an outside evaluator, trained to conduct a thorough evaluation. However, in most situations, BI librarians themselves can gather the data needed to present an informed picture of the program, its goals and achievements (Herman 1987; Shadish 1991).

Steps in Program Evaluation

- Conduct a needs assessment to establish what the goals of the program should be
- Compare the results of the needs assessment with the goals as stated. Note discrepancies
- Decide what evidence would demonstrate that the program is meeting its goal, does any of this evidence already exist?
- Determine what kinds of instruments will yield the evidence needed and how they can be administered
- Develop the instruments, pilot them, and revise
- Administer instruments
- Analyze the results
- Present the results to decision makers

Disseminating Results of An Evaluation

Throughout this chapter, "evaluation" has been defined as a systematic gathering of information in order to make decisions. Unless the information gathered is presented to those who make the decisions, then the evaluation has not served its purpose. A program evaluation will typically be initiated for a particular reason, and end with a final report, but every piece of evaluation documents some piece of the program. This important information should be reported to others.

Techniques for Disseminating Results

- Periodically send compilations of evaluations to other librarians, library and college administrators, the teaching faculty. A one page summary can present highlights while being brief and readable.
- For personnel decisions, have another person go through your evaluations and write a summary.
- Have classroom teachers administer post-instruction tests and surveys (they'll read them before sending them on).

- Always include an open-ended question on tests or surveys. Responses will not only give you more insight, but also provide quotes you can use.
- Write articles for your library newsletter or college newspapers.

Looking Ahead

Evaluating an instruction program, or parts of it, can have positive effects for you and your program. Use this chapter as a beginning to think about the information you need. Then use the other resources you have available, such as the books listed at the end of this chapter, or faculty on your own campus. What you learn can be used to your advantage and make a good instruction program even better.

For Further Reading

For overview information on various topics discussed in this chapter, see:

Encyclopedia of Educational Research. 6th ed. New York: Macmillan, 1992. Relevant articles: Attitude Measurement, Competency Testing, Dynamic Assessment, Evaluation of Programs, Measurement in Education, Performance Measurement, Reliability of Measurement, Teacher Evaluation, Test Construction, Validity of Test Interpretation and Use.

Encyclopedia of Sociology. New York: Macmillan, 1992.
Relevant articles: Measurement, Measurement Instruments, Sampling Procedures, Survey Research.

For help in teacher-made tests or writing test items, see basic texts on evaluation in education. Some examples:

Ebel, R. L., and D. A. Frisbie. *Essentials of Educational Measurement.* 4th ed. Englewood Cliffs, N.J.: Prentice-Hall, 1986.

Linn, R. L. *Educational Measurement.* 3d ed. New York: Macmillan, 1989.

Morris, L. L., et al. *How To Measure Performance and Use Tests.* Program Evaluation Kit, 2d ed., no. 7. Newbury Park, Calif.: Sage, 1987.

Thorndike, R. M. *Measurement and Evaluation in Education.* 5th ed. New York: Macmillan, 1991.

For an introduction to qualitative methods:

Bogdan, R. C., and S. K. Biklen. *Qualitative Research for Education: An Introduction to Theory and Methods*. 2d ed. Boston: Allyn and Bacon, 1992.

Patton, M. Q. *How to Use Qualitative Methods in Evaluation*. Program Evaluation Kit, 2d ed., no. 4. Newbury Park, Calif.: Sage, 1987.

For help in preparing surveys:

Henderson, M. E., et al. *How to Measure Attitudes*. Program Evaluation Kit, 2d ed., no. 6. Newbury Park, Calif.: Sage, 1987.

Payne, S. *The Art of Asking Questions*. Princeton, N. J.: Princeton University, 1951.
    A classic on the wording of questions, still in print after 40 years.

Schuman, H., and S. Presser. *Questions and Answers in Attitude Surveys: Experiments on Question Form, Wording and Context*. NY: Academic Press, 1981.

Sudman, S., and N. M. Bradburn. *Asking Questions: A Practical Guide to Question Design*. San Francisco: Jossey-Bass, 1987.

For background on how market researchers approach gathering information:

Boyd, H. W., et al. *Marketing Research: Text and Cases*. Homewood, Ill.: Irwin, 1988.

Breen, G. E., and .A. B. Blankenship *Do-It-Yourself Marketing Research*. 3d ed. New York: McGraw-Hill, 1989.

For information on program evaluation:

Herman, J. L., et al. *Evaluation Handbook*. Program Evaluation Kit, 2d ed., no. 1. Newbury Park, Calif: Sage, 1987.

Fitz-Gibbon, C. T., and L. L. Morris. *How To Design a Program Evaluation*. Program Evaluation Kit, 2d ed., no. 3. Newbury Park, Calif.: Sage, 1987.

Shadish, W. R. *Foundations of Program Evaluation: Theories of Practice.* Newbury Park, Calif.: Sage, 1991. Presents the history and theoretical basis of program evaluation.

For information on special aspects of evaluation:

Evaluating Bibliographic Instruction. Chicago: American Library Association, 1982. Designed as an introduction to evaluation theory and techniques for librarians. Contains chapters on goals and objectives, research design, data gathering instruments, and statistics.

Fitz-Gibbon, C. T., and L. L. Morris. *How to Analyze Data.* Program Evaluation Kit, 2d ed., no. 8. Newbury Park, Calif.: Sage, 1987. A basic explanation of common statistical procedures.

Morris, L. L., et al. *How to Communicate Evaluation Findings.* Program Evaluation Kit, 2d ed., no. 9. Newbury Park, CA: Sage, 1987 .

Examples of evaluation by BI librarians:

Adams, M., M. Loe, and M. Morey. *Evaluating a Library Instruction Program.* ERIC Document ED274 378. Bethesda, Md: ERIC Documentation Reproduction Service, 1987. Example of a program evaluation.

Hardesty, L., N. P. Lovrich, and J. Mannon. "Evaluating Library Instruction." *College and Research Libraries* 40 (July 1979): 309-317. Used a semantic differential scale to measure changes in student attitudes after instruction.

Harris, C. "Illuminative Evaluation of User Education Programs." *ASLIB Proceedings* 29 (October 1977): 348-362. Example of qualitative evaluation in BI.

King, D. N., and J. C. Ory. "Effects of Library Instruction on Student Research: A Case Study." *College and Research Libraries* 42, no. 1 (January 1981): 31-41. Used the examination of student papers to draw conclusions about student learning.

Knapp, P. *The Montieth College Library Experiment.* Metuchen, N.J.: Scarecrow Press, 1966. Chapter 4 describes an extensive performance measure developed to measure library skills.

Chapter Five

Setting Up and Managing a BI Program

Esther Grassian
University of California, Los Angeles

Are you a new Bibliographic Instruction coordinator? Do your job responsibilities include planning, coordinating, implementing and evaluating BI programs for your library? If so, you are probably feeling both excited and overwhelmed by your new responsibilities, as have many BI coordinators before you. Just as they did, you are wondering how you can get a handle on the current BI situation, not to mention past successes and failures, as well as options for the future. For example, how will you set up and manage BI programs which fit within departmental and campus goals, while at the same time maintaining staff support? How will you keep track of successes and shortcomings, and plan for evaluation and revision? How will you manage to coordinate BI through a team approach without the authority to require full or equal participation? And how will you achieve the ultimate goal—one or more required BI courses or BI as a component of one or more required courses?

It may help to remember that you are not alone. There are many people and resources available to help you study and revise existing programs, or develop new programs. If you are not fortunate enough to have taken a BI course in library school, you might want to begin by educating yourself, by learning about the wealth of approaches to BI through the reading materials listed in the appended bibliography, and by borrowing sample BI materials from the national BI depository LOEX (LOEX Clearing House, Eastern Michigan University Library, Ypsilanti, MI 48197, Director: Linda Shirato, (313) 487-0168, Publication: *LOEX News*, quarterly, Subscription: $50/year which includes membership and borrowing privileges).

In addition, through the course of your career as a BI Coordinator, you should make every effort to visit other libraries either on your campus or at other campuses to observe BI programs in action. And you can keep up to date on new developments in BI activities, programs, evaluation and more, by reading the quarterly *Research Strategies* and by subscribing to BI-L, the electronic discussion group for BI topics. BI-L describes itself by stating "BI-L is a computer conference dedicated to discussing ways of assisting library users in effectively and efficiently exploiting the resources available in and through the libraries of the 1990s. Contributions to the forum deal with the practical, theoretical, and technical aspects of what has been called Bibliographic Instruction, Library Use Instruction, Library Orientation, and several other names. We examine, explore, critique, appraise, and evaluate strategies, programs, and equipment that we have found to be valuable (or not) in working toward the goal of the self-sufficient library user " (See Appendix D).

You will also find much intellectual stimulation and enrichment throughout your career in BI from meeting and talking with other BI librarians at workshops, programs and conferences, such as the annual LOEX conference. Many BI librarians also attend local or regional BI clearinghouse meetings where they can network and share new ideas and experiences. If there is no clearinghouse in your area, you can start one by setting up a discussion group meeting for those interested in BI at your next state library association conference. If you ask attendees to bring along copies of their print and non-print instructional materials (handouts, pathfinders, etc.) you will have the beginnings of a healthy BI depository collection, which can be a valuable nearby resource.

You may want to think of this chapter as yet another resource to help you understand the many elements involved in coordinating BI programs, and to provide you with a variety of approaches to fulfilling your new responsibilities. The chapter begins by focusing on what you already know about instruction, proceeds to a study of the institution, the library and existing BI programs, continues with suggestions for planning change, and ends with a look to the future. This four-part structure should provide you with a general framework for planning, though you do not need to get complete answers for each section before proceeding to the next section. In fact, you will probably find the answers to some questions changing over time, sometimes abruptly and sometimes slowly. See Appendix A for guidance in sequencing if time is not a critical issue. When you need to work within a short time frame, on the other hand, you may need to investigate several different areas of concern at the same time. In any case, it would be wise to keep your finger on the pulse of your institution by monitoring changes in goals and top-level personnel.

Preliminary Inquiry

What do you already know about instruction?

What sorts of general instruction did you have when you were a student? Did you attend lectures, do exercises, fill out workbooks, watch instructional videotapes, participate in computer-assisted instruction, work with programmed texts, work on group projects, or complete in-class assignments?

And what sort of library instruction did you receive as a student? Did you go on a tour, attend an online public access catalog demo or a term paper clinic, complete a workbook, listen to a library lecture, complete a library exercise or watch a library instruction videotape? At this point, you might want to make a list of the types of instruction you yourself have experienced, and compare it to the types of instruction listed in Chapter Three. Later, when you make suggestions or decisions on BI programs, you might want to keep in mind the types of instruction you felt were most effective for yourself and others you knew when you were a student.

Step One: Institutional and Library-Wide Inquiry, and Study of Existing BI Program(s)

How should you study existing programs?

The following series of questions and suggestions should help you as you examine your BI program(s). In answering these questions, you will become familiar with the "culture" of your institution, its politics, its commitment to the library and its readiness for change.   The suggestions and hints may make your job easier if they fit your circumstances and if you remember to work as closely as possible with other staff members to coordinate decisions. You might want to use a looseleaf notebook, a card file or a database management program along with this chapter, in order to keep track of information for your institution. If you find it easier and faster to keep track of and retrieve information by using a computerized system, rather than by writing it down, you might look into utilizing a software package with full-text indexing capability. If the program allows for free-text records, you can develop your own system for recording BI-related information, similar to notebook or card file records. Hyper-links can hook data or records together, as well.

1. What are the overall goals of your institution?
Check the institution's course catalog for a general goals statement. Find out what the general requirements are for all students. A library component would be ideal, for example, as a build-in element of a "writing-across-the-curriculum" requirement.

2. What are the institutional politics?
With a copy of the institution's top organization chart in hand, you will be able to see where the library fits in the campus organization, and to whom the library director reports. This will give you an idea of the formal reporting structure and administrative network. Informal contacts can also be quite useful. You might want to interview library administrators about formal and informal networking opportunities throughout the institution.

Try talking with your colleagues about the history of BI involvement with various departments on campus. What type of BI do participating departments prefer? Has their participation been voluntary or solicited by the library? You might want to consider contacting these departments first when putting out feelers about new or revised BI programs, simply because they have shown an interest in BI programs in the past.

Is there a media center, instructional center or learning resource center and does it have a relationship to the library? It would be a good idea to try to build bridges between the library and this department. The media center might be able to prepare handouts and course materials, or even help create library instruction videos.

It would also be helpful to establish or continue a good relationship with the computing center and the Education department. The Education department (and the media center) might be able to help librarians hone their instructional skills by serving as consultants, or offering workshops on teaching techniques and classroom management. And the campus computing center might provide training in software and hardware use, both for creating instructional materials and to help train users.

3. What are the library's goals?

Does the library aim to serve all comers, or has it established service priorities, both for primary and non-primary users? How do these priorities affect BI? For example, does your library offer the full range of BI services and programs to high school students, extension students, or students from other colleges and universities? Do the library's service goals for faculty differ from those for other groups? What are the service goals for dorm residents, as opposed to commuters, and for part-time or reentry students?

Is there an overall BI Coordinator for all campus libraries, or a BI Advisory Committee? Who is on the BI Advisory Committee? Have they set general BI goals and objectives for the library at large based on library service goals? Is the library administration generally favorable to their recommendations?

Is access to certain materials restricted? If you do offer BI programs for your non-primary users, do they have free access to the full range of library resources—e.g., journal article databases?

Is there a campus-wide outreach program to other schools---e.g., Advanced Placement high school students, transfer students? If so, how is the library involved?

Is there a "Summer Bridge Program"—i.e., where students who will be enrolled in the Fall get special summer orientation and training? How does the library participate?

Do annual reports use BI statistics to indicate that the library is working toward a particular goal?

4. What BI programs are currently in place?

Learn all you can about your institution's BI programs, formal and informal, and make note of any written *goals and objectives* for each of them. If there are no written goals and objectives, interview the participants and administrators to determine the goals and objectives, and make separate notes on each program.

> **HINT:** It is very important to check the completeness of the BI program list, and your understanding of their goals and objectives with the reference/BI staff and the administration, before proceeding. This step is especially important if you are new to the institution, because in spite of all your efforts you may have missed an important piece of BI or institutional history, or misunderstood the goals and objectives of existing BI programs. If there are no written goals and objectives, brainstorming sessions would be a good way to establish them (Van Gunder 1981).

How do the existing programs work (Modus Operandi)?

Are there *training manuals, teaching materials,* or other *descriptive items* regarding these programs, including *marketing* and *publicity* materials, as well as instructions for record-keeping?

It would be helpful to make an *outline of the program's operational steps,* and be sure to take note of any individual variations. For example, one program's operational steps might be:

a. 50 classes of 25 students each are scheduled for the BI classroom at the beginning of each quarter, spread out over a period of 3 weeks.
b. Librarian meets class in classroom, gives very brief introduction, hands out blank cards.
c. Students have 2 minutes to write library-related question on cards.
d. Librarian collects cards, reads questions to the class and answers each question on the spot.
e. Class views 10-minute BI videotape.
f. Class leaves classroom to do 20-minute hands-on BI exercise at online public catalog (opac) with the help of the librarian and a "back-up" (additional librarian or trained para-professional).

5. How are the budget and staffing patterns for BI handled?

Is there a separate *BI budget* ? If there is one, check to see whether or not it includes indirect costs, such as staff time. If there is no separate BI budget, what is the procedure for requesting funding for BI equipment, photocopying, staffing, etc.? If items must be requested through proposals in the form of memos, it would be helpful to look at copies of previous proposals, including those not funded. In some institutions, you may need to do an annual BI budget request—in others, you may expect to receive the same budget (or materials and equipment) unless you specifically request something else.

> **HINT: Limit your proposal to two pages.** Include a statement of the problem or need, proposed solution, pros, cons, costs, and a conclusion. Share your draft proposal with your colleagues before sending it on to the administration.

What is the BI *staffing pattern* ? What sort of authority does the BI coordinator have in terms of assigning instructional duties, allocating the BI budget, preparing the BI schedule, etc.? Do you report to a Head of Reference, or directly to a Head of Public Services or the Library Director? Will you have staff or students assigned to the program? Is there any chance of getting a library school student to serve as a BI intern?

Try to estimate through written materials, through observation or through interviews, the direct and indirect *staff time* and the *level of staff* required to run the programs.

What *level of commitment* is each staff member expected to maintain during "on- and-off-seasons"?

6. What technology is available for BI programming?

What sort of *technology* does the library use *to set up and manage* the program? BI statistics, for example, may be required for your library's annual report. Such statistics can also be useful in writing proposals for additional funding, especially if you keep track of the requests you could not fill, as well as those you did. In addition, if you intend to sequence instruction, reporting by department would be quite useful.

If you are in a large institution with numerous BI programs serving large user populations, you might want to consider developing a log or standard BI statistics reporting form, and using a software package to keep track of and report BI statistics. There are a number of sophisticated, as well as simpler software packages, which could be utilized to keep track of BI statistics. For example, you might ask someone with dBase experience to set up a simple menu-driven statistics tracking program. On the other hand, spreadsheet programs such as Quattro and Excel allow you to enter and manipulate a large variety of statistics. Quattro, Excel and dBase are currently used widely; however, other useful software packages may be developed in the future.

What sort of *technology do audiovisual program participants use*? Does the program involve use of audiovisual equipment and materials (e.g.,VCR), computer hardware or software? If so, who is responsible for troubleshooting hardware and software, reordering and replacing missing bulbs or other parts? Is there a maintenance checklist? Who is responsible for maintenance?

If you are at a large campus, is there a *list of instructional equipment* available for loan from other libraries on campus? Can the library rent equipment on a temporary basis, if necessary? Is there a list of library-owned instructional equipment, with serial numbers or property numbers? How and when is equipment or software replaced or upgraded?

7. What evaluation methods are currently in place?

Inquire about *evaluation* and *revision* procedures. How are programs evaluated? How often they are evaluated? When did the last evaluation occur? What were the results? See Chapter 4, on Evaluation for further information.

It is important to share all of this information with the BI Advisory Committee (if there is one), to verify facts and to generate discussion on future possible changes.

Step Two: Inquiry Into Change

How do you plan for future change?

1. What are the first questions you need to ask about change?

Is there a mandate for change? If there is a mandate for change, who has mandated the change and why, and who is responsible for carrying it out? What kind of change do staff, faculty, users and administration want?

a. **Tinker with current program**—i.e., minor revision with little or no shift in goals, objectives or format, such as selecting different search terms for an opac exercise, clarifying workbook instructions, decreasing number of staff needed to operate the program, or incorporating information about new opac enhancements.

b. **Major overhaul of current program**—i.e., a major shift in goals, objectives, or format, such as a shift from an intensive one-shot lecture approach to a self-paced workbook, or a shift from teaching the mechanics of using one opac to locate books and periodicals, to teaching the concept of a database, and then introducing a variety of book, article and periodical title databases available through one or more opacs or workstations.

c. **Discard current program in favor of new approach.**

d. **Add one or more new programs.** You can get ideas for new questions or search terms, assignments, BI videotapes and more by borrowing sample materials from LOEX. A BI intern can also be of great help in coming up with ideas for assignments, and in doing some of the legwork.

2. How much lead time is available for planning?

Do any or all of these groups feel that a *needs assessment* would be in order? For example, the user population may have changed, there may have been major changes to library technology, or there may be desire to focus on new needs or previously unmet needs.

Do staff, faculty, users or administration want to set different *goals and objectives* or different means for achieving the same goals and objectives? Or do they simply want to add something new?

It is important to find out before you proceed what your authority and responsibilities are in making change. Keep in mind that you will probably not be making these decisions on your own. You may very well need to work with the BI Advisory Committee, other reference librarians, other BI Coordinators, the department head, top level administrators, and others, and come to a consensus. You may then need to put your consensus recommendations on paper in the form of a proposal.

Step Three: Planning and Shepherding Change

1. How should you approach a minor revision?

First, determine that the revision is indeed minor, and as such, will require little or no change to program goals and objectives.

Estimate the staff time, materials and cost needed to accomplish the revision. Remember that even minor revisions to a program may take some time to develop, so be sure to plan for them as far in advance as possible.

Enlist your colleagues' help, if necessary, or ask for some student assistant time to develop changes to print or non-print materials or lecture matter.

2. How should you prepare proposals for a major overhaul or new program?

Be sure to include an explanation of how and why any new goals and objectives differ from the old ones.

Prepare at least two proposals for each type of BI program you would like to offer—one with basic funding and one with extra funding. Your proposal for basic funding, for example, might include the sale of workbooks which would not only pay for publication costs, but could also support additional staff or student help for correction, help at the reference desk, and purchase of equipment and materials to support the program. You would need to ask for extra funding up front for initial staffing and printing costs, which could then be repaid as workbooks are sold. Alternatively, you may wish to ask for support from departments or other groups receiving instruction, at least in the form of printing and duplicating costs. Extra funding might cover the cost of a more attractive cover or better binding for workbooks, or a videotape with dialogue, as opposed to voiceover, for example.

You may want to request software in your BI program proposal. If you request software for end-users, make sure you factor into your proposal a sufficient number of workstations to run the software, as well as enough electrical outlets for them. Some commercial BI software packages can even be customized for your library. One example of such a program currently in use is an interactive Macintosh CAI program, "Research Assistant," created by Ann F. Bevilacqua (Bevilacqua 1989). Check with any available instructional media experts and "techies" regarding software and hardware which you might want to use to create your own computerized BI program.

What happens when the technology changes? If your BI program includes instruction in the use of your opac, CD-ROMs, or other databases, you will need to keep very close tabs on program and coverage changes. In fact, you would be wise to expect change and be prepared for quick revision and staff retraining or updating especially in this age of geometric technological change.

Consider calling for volunteers to help out with your BI program, keeping in mind that dependence on volunteers can be risky. If you do invite volunteers to participate, you will need to train them and have a backup plan in case there are no-shows.

For any proposal involving new or revised programs, remember to build in time for *program development, as well as retraining* for the new program(s).

No matter which type of proposal you prepare, always check with all staff involved before presenting it to the administration. And keep in mind throughout that there may be an impact on reference service, no matter which BI program is adopted. The impact may come in the form of staff inundated and annoyed with "BI program questions" at the reference desk, or professional staff available to put in fewer reference hours, or too exhausted from a heavy BI load to provide good reference service. If you do not have para-professionals or students staffing the reference desk, there may also be increased pressure to do so, so that professionals can be released to do more BI. This can create quite a tricky situation if a library's BI goals come in conflict with the library's overall service goals regarding the level and quality of service.

It would be extremely helpful to bring these potential problem areas out into the open by discussing them with the library staff before they happen. Just talking about BI-related problems and issues at staff meetings can be cathartic, especially when staff can work together to come up with solutions. In any case, it would probably be helpful to communicate your concerns to library administration, and ask for clarification regarding the library's general goals as opposed to its BI goals. It is important to keep in mind here that there may be disagreement on what it takes to fulfill the library's service goals, or even what varying levels of service mean. In the end, the library staff may need to come to terms with the fact that these differences of opinion exist and that library administration will make the final decision on where to allocate scarce resources, including people.

3. How will you train staff for lecture-type BI?

It is important to prepare rehearsal sessions for those who will be doing lectures.

Be supportive throughout these rehearsal sessions and welcome diverse approaches. In fact, these sessions will probably work best if you treat them as two-way learning experiences. Librarian-lecturers-to-be will see you demonstrate a BI session in your teaching style. In turn, you may learn other approaches to covering the same concepts, from them. It would probably help if each person has an outline of the subject matter that needs to be covered, along with a lecture evaluation checklist. See Appendix B for a sample checklist.

When you do a demo-session yourself, it might help to ask for constructive comments based on two questions: "What did you like?" and "How would you do it differently?". You might then want to ask some of the attendees to do a brief demo-session, as well.

Understand that there will be some staff members who feel uncomfortable lecturing, so be sure not to embarrass anyone or single out a reluctant colleague. These individuals may wish to contribute to the library's BI efforts in other equally valid and valuable ways. For example, such individuals might be interested in developing a workbook program, pathfinders, handouts, or exercises, and might also be willing to spend extra time at the reference desk to release others for classroom teaching.

You must be careful, on the other hand, not to exploit these librarians by having them staff the reference desk for hours on end while others are off spending most of their time teaching. It is important to keep two things in mind here: First, the end result of effective BI is not to decrease the number of questions asked at a reference desk, but to raise them to higher levels of complexity. The more complex the question, the greater the need for a professional to answer it. Second, in effect, those who staff the reference desk are doing much one-on-one teaching, and may become just as stressed and burned out as those who teach endless hours in the classroom. In any case, if unequal participation becomes a morale problem, it should be discussed with the department head or the Library Director. See bibliography items on learning styles (Gagne 1988; Hergenhahn 1982; Schimeck 1988; Stupex 1988; Wheldall and Glynn 1984), and training methods (Fournies 1978; Blue Ridge Summit 1988; Phillips 1987; Robinson 1983).

> **Hint**: It would be helpful if you could incorporate information about *body language and cultural differences* among users and staff in your rehearsal sessions. See bibliography items on body language and cultural differences (Copeland 1988; Poyatos 1988; Scheflen 1972). If you do not have enough expertise in these areas yourself, you might want to look into having a guest speaker at your basic training session, or at a special workshop set up at a later date. Again, you may need to prepare a written proposal to the administration for special workshops or guest speakers.

4. What sort of implementation training will you need to prepare for non-lecture-type BI?

You may also need to prepare *training sessions* to handle *CAI* and *print* BI programs (e.g., self-paced workbooks). If you do, it would help to have a written procedures manual, including a rationale and methodology for staggering due dates for large classes, as well as sample forms needed for photocopying or purchasing supplies. You might want to divide the training session into two parts, with one part focused on content and the other on program mechanics.

> **Hint:** In the content portion of the session, it would probably be a good idea to emphasize the fact that in spite of the repetitive nature of some questions to us, the *answers are always new to the questioner*. It might also help to remind staff that *most people learn best by doing*.

5. How do you incorporate evaluation and revision in training sessions?

In all training sessions, you would do well to explain the *evaluation* and *revision process,* as well as staff and user input into this process. It would also be a good idea to remind staff and administrators that particularly in the technological age, BI programs cannot be "set in stone." They must be flexible and designed to accommodate change as libraries and society change (Light 1990; Lubans 1974 and see Chapter Four on Evaluation).

6. What sort of advance planning is necessary for scheduling and creation or revision of BI materials?

Advance planning is essential for quality instruction. One of the most difficult things you will need to do as a BI Coordinator is to say "No" to last-minute requests for instruction. It is important to be as diplomatic as possible when you do need to turn down requests for instruction, and suggest other possible places, times and dates for instructional sessions. If you do not turn down last minute requests for instruction, you may find such demands increasing, with an accompanying decrease in the quality of your instruction, and a loss of respect for your need to prepare.

Do your best to *schedule BI activities, rooms, photocopying and equipment use in advance*. You will need to do this in coordination with the instructor, academic department, or other group(s) request for instruction, as well as with staff participating in requesting instruction.

> **Hint**: A *calendar and signup sheet* specifically for instructional rooms, equipment and activities are essential, especially if you are sharing rooms and equipment, or using volunteers.

Plan ahead for printed instructional materials design (including paper color and layout), (Collier and Kay 1989; Ketcham 1958) testing, revision, copying, collating and stapling. Remember, if you need anything new on a large scale, you may need to write up a special proposal in the form of a memo as much as a year in advance. Check on the availability of general library guides and opac handouts for distribution at BI sessions or inclusion in BI packets.

Test each new BI product on naive users. Pay careful attention to any problems they encounter and keep revising until your products are simple, brief and crystal clear. *Plan very far ahead in designing a BI videotape or CAI*. Begin with brainstorming sessions about goals and objectives, then brainstorming sessions about plot, characters, etc. (Smith 1988).

7. How should you go about publicizing and marketing your BI programs? *Publicize* the BI program(s) to the extent that staff is available to handle the demand, but also be prepared for low initial participation.

Be prepared to make assertive contact with faculty and departments (e.g., Freshman Summer Program) regarding your BI programs and services. Some departments may only need written reminders far in advance, while others may require endless phone calls. You might consider e-mail communication, as well, if you have that capability at your institution.

Be a BI subversive. Try to get *academic department support* for the BI program by making strategic alliances with faculty at every opportunity--the Faculty Club, committee meetings, social gatherings, etc.

It is important to stress the importance of BI for all students, particularly in the electronic age. If your institution has a required freshman course on "campus life," you might want to lobby for an introductory BI component. At the same time, you can work toward offering more advanced BI at different points—e.g., term paper clinics for sophomores through seniors, and advanced research methods for graduate students and faculty. This sort of "cradle-to-grave," sequential, or "tiered" instructional program could be designed to fit in with the institution's goals, the library's goals and even the accreditation process.

You might also consider marketing your wares to instructors with problem assignments for large numbers of students. Try contacting the instructor who created the assignment, and offer to work together to create a more effective assignment. Point out to the instructor that by providing a more effective assignment, the students' papers may be more interesting to read, and research materials will be preserved. This can be a delicate interchange, as we want to encourage these faculty members to continue focusing on the library, but also to make the experience a less frustrating and negative one for the students.

Faculty members are themselves often anxious and insecure about library use, particularly if they are computer-phobic. So how do you handle this ticklish problem—how do you relieve the instructor's anxiety, and at the same time make the instructor feel comfortable both in using library resources and making library assignments?

Diplomacy is the key. You will need to walk a fine line between welcoming the instructor's desire to introduce students to the research process, and your desire to provide an effective and nonfrustrating experience for the students. The California Clearinghouse on Library Instruction has created a useful set of guidelines for faculty-created library assignments. Contact LOEX for a copy of the guidelines.

> **Hint:** In some cases it might help to point out that the instructor will probably end up with more interesting and interdisciplinary papers if the students have an increased number of topics and sources from which to choose. You might want to point out, too, the *vast and ever-changing array of electronic resources* available to students and faculty alike, and the fact that you would be excited about any opportunity to teach students new ways of finding information on a topic. The instructor might also welcome such an offer to teach, and may learn a bit in the process, as well.

There are many ways to publicize a BI program, both traditional and non-traditional. Traditional publicity and marketing can include memos or letters to faculty, signs, posters or banners in the library about upcoming instructional sessions. Circulation students can put bookmarks into books as they are checked out. The library can pay for an ad in the campus newspaper.

Some non-traditional methods may also get your BI program some much-needed attention. You can send coupons to faculty offering a "free consultation" on a topic/reference source of their choice (Loyola Marymount, CA). You can offer faculty "update" sessions (University of California, Berkeley), to acquaint them with new electronic reference sources, and then offer to do the same for their students. You can use catchy titles for your BI sessions—e.g., "M.O.L.E. (Moffitt Orientation and Library Education—University of California, Berkeley). Contact LOEX for other examples of interesting program titles.

8. What are the main areas of "people-related" concern in discarding an older BI program, or setting up and managing a new or revised one?

There may be *resistance to change* from staff, faculty, users or administration, particularly if there are plans to discard or do a major overhaul to one or more programs. Change, while exciting, can also be extremely threatening and stressful. You can alleviate the threatening aspects of change by maintaining complete and continuous two-way communication, by utilizing brainstorming techniques which involve the entire staff, and by directing strongly vented feelings toward positive action. In this way, the participants will help create the plan and will be more likely to "buy into" it. Keep in mind that true brainstorming begins with encouraging participants to voice all sorts of comments and ideas in a non-judgmental setting (VanGunder 1981).

Be sensitive to the *stress* and *burnout* levels of the staff. There are a number of steps you can take to minimize stress and burnout (Caputo 1991).

a. Encourage equal participation in BI programs and activities.
b. Show appreciation verbally and in public, for staff efforts and successes at all levels, and encourage administrators to do the same.
c. Work toward administrative flexibility regarding comp-time and vacation during slow periods. Staff will need a chance to recover from the intensity of high-pressure BI and reference periods.
d. Show appreciation in material ways—write a thank-you letter to each person who helped out with the program, including staff; have an "end-of-the-BI-term" party or pot-luck lunch, and unwind.
e. Encourage administrators to include BI activity and contributions in performance reviews.

Be sensitive to *diversity issues* . Check, and regularly revise examples used in BI sessions and materials to reflect the diverse nature of society. Contact LOEX or your local or regional BI clearinghouse for sample materials and examples reflecting diversity issues (Mensching 1989).

Beware the "shifting sands" of *administrative commitment*. Good intentions and enthusiasm may not be able to overcome one or more years of budget cuts and staff shortages. Be prepared to defend the cost-effectiveness of your BI programs, while keeping an open mind about change. Also, remember that administrators come and go, and with them, for better or worse, go their BI priorities.

Step Four: Look Ahead

How can you promote a flexible environment, conducive to change?

Be prepared to *reevaluate, revise or discard programs* as needs change—user needs, staff needs or administrative needs. Keep in mind that long-term BI programs sometimes run in cycles—they live for a while, they grow and change, and sometimes they die.

Be prepared to *be flexible,* to adjust to change, and to welcome it as a time to stretch and be creative.

For the best of all possible BI worlds, try to *offer a variety of programs* to meet the inevitable variety of user needs and learning styles, and to allow for differing staff interests and abilities.

In this chapter you have reviewed your knowledge of instruction, learned how to study existing BI programs, and how to plan for the future. This is just a beginning, but it should provide you with some basic skills for navigating what may seem like uncharted BI waters. To become a good BI "navigator," you will need to work with the rest of the staff as well as the administration in evaluating your institution's needs and making informed recommendations regarding the path your BI program(s) should take. Though the journey may be both exciting and hazardous, you now have a basic map of the route to help you steer a true course.

References

Body Language & Cultural Differences

Copeland, Lennie. "Valuing Diversity, Part 1: Making the Most of Cultural Difference at the Workplace." *Personnel* 65, no.6 (June 1988): 52-60.

Poyatos, Fernando, ed. *Cross-Cultural Perspectives in Non-Verbal Communication.* Lewiston, N. Y., Toronto: Hogrefe, 1988.

Scheflen, Albert E. *Body Language and Social Order: Communication as Behavioral Control.* Englewood Cliffs, N.J.: Prentice-Hall, 1972.

Brainstorming

VanGunder, Arthur B. *Techniques of Structured Problem Solving.* New York: Van Nostrand Reinhold, 1981.

Diversity & BI

Mensching, Teresa B., ed. *Reaching and Teaching Diverse Library User Groups.* Papers presented at the 16th National LOEX Conference, Bowling Green University, May 5-6, 1988. Ann Arbor, Mich.: Pierian Press, 1989.

Evaluation & Revision

Evaluating Bibliographic Instruction: A Handbook. Chicago, Ill.: Bibliographic Instruction Section, Association of College and Research Libraries, American Library Association, 1983.

Light, Richard L. *Harvard Assessment Seminars.* First Report. Cambridge, Mass.: Harvard University, 1990.

Lubans, John, Jr. "Evaluating Library-User Education Programs." In *Educating the Library User,* edited by John Lubans, 232-253. New York: Bowker, 1974.

Handout Design

Collier, David and Kay Floyd. *Ready-to-Use Layouts for Desktop Design*. Cincinnati, Ohio: North Light Books, 1989.

Ketcham, Howard. *Color Planning*. New York: Harper & Brothers, 1958.

Learning Styles

Gagne, Robert Mills. *The Conditions of Learning*. 4th ed. New York: Holt, Rinehart & Winston, 1985.

Hergenhahn, B. R. *An Introduction to Theories of Learning*. Englewood Cliffs, N.J.: Prentice-Hall, 1982.

Schmeck, Ronald R., ed. *Learning Strategies & Learning Styles*. New York: Plenum, 1988.

Stipek, Deborah. *Motivation to Learn: From Theory to Practice*. Englewood Cliffs, N.J.: Prentice-Hall, 1988.

Wheldall, Kevin, and Ted Glynn. *Effective Classroom Learning*. New York: Basil Blackwell, 1989.

Stress & Burnout

Caputo, Judith S. *Stress and Burnout in Library Service*. Phoenix, Ariz: Oryx Press, 1991.

Technology & BI

Bevilacqua, Ann F. *Research Assistant*. (a software program) Manchester, Conn: Upper Broadway Bodega, 1989. For further information about "Research Assistant," contact Ann F. Bevilacqua, Upper Broadway Bodega, Box 855, Manchester, CT 06040, (203) 647-8104.

MacDonald, Linda Brew, et al. *Teaching Technologies in Libraries: a Practical Guide*. Boston: G.K. Hall, 1991.

Training Methods

Fournies, Ferdinand F. *Coaching for Improved Work Performance.* New York: Van Nostrand, 1978.

Phillips, Jack J. *Recruiting, Training and Retaining New Employees: Managing the Transition from College to Work.* San Francisco: Jossey-Bass, 1987.

Robinson, J. C. *Developing Managers Through Behavior Modeling.* Austin, Texas: Learning Concepts, 1983.

Why Employees Don't Do What They're Supposed to Do and What to Do About It. Blue Ridge Summit, Penn: Liberty House, 1988.

Recommended Readings

These readings were selected with the beginning bibliographic instruction librarian in mind. The list is meant to be selective and practical, rather than completely comprehensive.

Baker, Betsy, and Litzinger, Mary Ellen, eds. *The Evolving Educational Mission of the Library*. Chicago: Association of College and Research Libraries, 1992.

> The 1989 BIS-sponsored think tank identified issues that were important strategically for bibliographic instruction librarians and these issues are covered in this book. Topics include librarian roles on campus, new educational constituencies, the information explosion, and information literacy.

Beaubien, Anne K., et. al. *Learning the Library: Concepts and Methods for Effective Bibliographic Instruction*. New York: Bowker, 1982.

> A comprehensive, classic work that covers how to set instructional objectives, research problem analysis, library administrative climate, costs of bibliographic instruction programs, and needs analysis.

Brottman, May, and Mary Loe. *The LIRT Library Instruction Handbook*. Englewood, Colo.: Libraries Unlimited, 1990.

> Covers planning and managing an instruction program and applies library instruction in academic libraries, public libraries, school media centers, and special libraries, and includes a detailed bibliography.

Carlson, D., and B. B. Miller. "Librarians and Teaching Faculty: Partners in Bibliographic Instruction." *College and Research Libraries* 45 (November 1984): 483-491.

> Focuses on the key factors of course-related bibliographic instruction, which are: administrative issues; coordination and scheduling of class materials; faculty's crucial role; maintaining consistent programs; and the ability of users to transfer knowledge to a variety of courses.

Chadley, O., and J. Gavyrck. "Bibliographic Instruction Trends in Research Libraries." *Research Strategies* 7 (Summer 1989): 106-113.

> Survey of 72 ARL Libraries to assess how bibliographic instruction programs have changed from 1983-1988. Results of survey indicate that instructional programs are now standard offerings by research libraries.

Curtis, Ruth V., and C. Herbert Carson. "The Application of Motivational Design to Bibliographic Instruction." *Research Strategies* 9 (Summer 1991): 130-138.

Utilizes Keller's ARCS Model of motivational design to illustrate that motivation is the key to successful BI.

Dusenbury, Carolyn, et al., eds. *Read This First: An Owner's Guide to the New Model Statement of Objectives for Academic Bibliographic Instruction.* Chicago: Bibliographic Instruction Section, Association of College and Research Libraries, 1991.

The purpose of the model statement of objectives is to "generate thinking in the discipline of bibliographic instruction concerning the direction of existing instructional programs," p. 5. This work reprints the model statement, analyzes it, and provides six working examples of the model statement as applied to BI programs.

Elsbernd, M. E. Rutledge, N. F. Campbell, and T. L. Wesley. "The Best of OPAC Instruction: A Selected Guide for the Beginner." *Research Strategies* 8 (Winter 1990): 28-36.

A literature review of the online public access catalog (OPAC) from 1980-1989. The articles reviewed cover the value of instruction, and how to teach; faculty education; and serving remote users.

Evaluating Bibliographic Instruction: A Handbook. Edited by ACRL Bibliographic Instruction Section, Association of College and Research Libraries. Chicago: American Library Association, 1983.

Chapters cover the use of evaluation, goals and objectives, research designs, data gathering instruments, and statistical analysis. Also features a well-chosen bibliography and a glossary.

Frick, Elizabeth. "Qualitative Evaluation of User Education Programs: The Best Choice?" *Research Strategies* 8 (Winter 1990): 4-13.

Compares qualitative and quantitative approaches to evaluate library instruction, and identifies when a particular approach is appropriate.

Hopkins, F. L.. "A Century of Bibliographic Instruction: The Historical Claim to Professional and Academic Legitimacy." *College and Research Libraries* 43, no. 3 (May 1982): 192-198.

Makes a strong case for bibliographic instruction.

Johnson, Judy. "Application of Learning Theory to Bibliographic Instruction: An Annotated Bibliography." *Research Strategies* 4 (Summer 1986): 139-141.

Learning theory and its applications to bibliographic instruction are found in this annotated bibliography. Includes materials published within the last ten years, and earlier standard works.

Kerbel, Sandra Sandor. "Confessions of a Novice." *Journal of Academic Librarianship* 8, no.6 (January 1983): 354-355.

Recommended for beginning bibliographic instruction librarians.

Kirkendall, Carolyn, ed. *Bibliographic Instruction and the Learning Process: Theory, Style and Motivation.* Ann Arbor, Mich.: Pierian Press, 1984.

A sound introduction to learning theory.

Kuhlthau, Carol C. "Inside the Search Process: Information Seeking from the User's Perspective." *Journal of the American Society for Information Science* 42 (January 1991): 361-371.

Discusses the user's Information Search Process (ISP), from 5 studies which investigate experiences of users seeking information, which indicates a gap between a user seeking information, the information system, and the library's pattern of providing information.

Lawton, Bethany. "Library Instruction Needs Assessment: Designing Survey Instruments." *Research Strategies* 8 (Summer 1989): 119-128.

Three different questionnaires were given to the students, faculty and staff at Gallaudet University as a means of assessing the needs of these groups to formulate a new BI program. Responses received from the questionnaire were used to create a newly tailored bibliographic instruction program.

Learning to Teach: Workshops on Instruction, Chicago: Bibliographic Instruction Section. Association of American College and Research Libraries, 1989.

Nine modules cover how to teach instruction librarians to teach.

McCarthy, Constance. "Library Instruction: Observations from the Reference Desk." *RQ* 22 (Fall 1992): 36-41.

> Highlights how guilt, overconfidence and indignation negatively impact a user to effective use of a research library, and how successful BI can bring about positive results, such as trust and adventurousness.

Mellon, Constance. *Bibliographic Instruction: The Second Generation.* Littleton, Colo.: Libraries Unlimited, 1987.

> Compilation of writings from individuals who were instrumental in the development of academic bibliographic instruction. Topics discussed include understanding the user, specialized BI and future directions of library instruction.

Miller, M., and B. D. Bratton. "Instructional Design: Increasing the Effectiveness of Bibliographic Instruction." *College and Research Libraries* 49, no.6 (November 1988): 545-549.

> Instructional design is presented as a tool to create an effective BI program. The components of such a program are: learners, learning objectives, subject content, teaching methods, evaluation of the learning process, and instructional design methods.

Nipp, Deanna. "Back to Basics: Integrating CD ROM Instruction with Standard User Education." *Research Strategies* 9 (Winter 1991): 41-47.

> Discusses the importance of bibliographic instruction for CD ROM databases and how this service has been integrated into a variety of instructional methods.

Oberman, Cerise and Katina Strauch. *Theories of Bibliographic Education: Designs for Teaching.* New York: Bowker, 1982.

> In addition to other topics, covers course-related instruction, guided design and workbooks.

Organizing and Managing a Library Instruction Program: Checklists. Rev. ed. Association of College and Research Libraries, Bibliographic Instruction Section, Continuing Education Committee. Chicago: Association of College and Research Libraries, 1986.

> Checklist provides guidelines for establishing a bibliographic instruction program for the following areas: preliminary planning; developing goals and objectives; creating and maintaining internal and external support; how to administer the program; types of instructional methods/materials; training; and

evaluation of the program.

Pastine, Maureen, and Bill Katz. *Integrating Library Use Skills Into the General Education Curriculum*. New York: Hawthorn Press, 1989.

Reichel, Mary and Mary Anne Ramey, eds. *Conceptual Frameworks for Bibliographic Education: Theory into Practice*. Littleton, Colo.: Libraries Unlimited, 1987.

Roberts, Anne F., and Susan G. Blandy. *Library Instruction for Librarians*. Englewood, Colo: Libraries Unlimited, 1989.

Covers the history of bibliographic instruction, education for librarians, deciding on a program and the format, maintaining a program, and instructional programs for specific groups.

Sheridan, Joan. "The Reflective Librarian: Some Observations on Bibliographic Instruction in the Academic Library." *Journal of Academic Librarianship* 16, no.1 (1990): 22-26.

Discusses collaborative learning and includes descriptions of methods and techniques for implementing collaborative learning in BI sessions.

Svinicki, Marilla D., and Barbara A. Schwartz. *Designing Instruction for Library Users: A Practical Guide*. New York: Marcel Dekker, 1988.

Written for librarians responsible for teaching BI. Describes a system for categorizing instructional methods; types of instruction; designing and sequencing instruction; and learning theory. Applies this design to eight case studies and offers suggestions for evaluating a program, and concludes with some suggestions for designing a program.

Setting Up and Managing a BI Program
Outline of Steps

Preliminary Inquiry

What do you already know about instruction?

Step One: Institutional and Library-wide Inquiry & Study of Existing BI Program(s)

What are the overall goals of your institution?
What are the institutional politics?
What are the library's goals?
What BI programs are currently in place?
— What are their goals and objectives?
— How do they work (Modus Operandi)?

Step Two: Inquiry into Change

Who will decide, and how?
What kind of change do decision-makers want?
What are the time constraints?

Step Three: Planning and Shepherding Change

How should you plan for a minor revision, a major revision, a newly added program or a discarded program?
What sort of training will you need to prepare for and implement new or revised programs?
How will you incorporate evaluation and revision in training sessions and in programs?
What sort of advance planning is necessary for scheduling and creation or revision of BI materials?
How should you go about publicizing and marketing your new or revised BI programs?
What are the main areas of "people-related" concern in discarding an older BI program, or setting up and managing a new or revised one?

Step Four: A Look Ahead

How can you promote a flexible environment, conducive to change?

Checklist for Evaluating Lecture Presentations*

Establishing and Maintaining Contact With Attendees
_____ Greeted attendees
_____ Set ground rules for participation and questioning
_____ Noted and responded to signs of puzzlement, boredom, curiosity, etc.
_____ Varied the pace of the presentation
_____ Spoke at a rate which allowed attendees to take notes as necessary

Organization of Lecture Content
_____Stated purpose of the presentation
_____ Presented brief overview of content
_____ Asked questions to determine whether too much or too little presented
_____ Presented examples to clarify new, abstract or difficult ideas
_____ Explicitly stated relationships among ideas
_____ Periodically summarized the most important ideas
_____ In concluding, restated what students were expected to learn

Presentation Style
_____Voice could be easily heard
_____ Voice was raised or lowered for emphasis
_____ Speech was neither too formal nor too casual
_____ Speech fillers, e.g. "ahmm," were not distracting
_____ Rate of speech was neither too fast nor too slow
_____ Maintained eye contact
_____ Listened carefully to comments and questions
_____ Facial and body movements did not contradict speech or expressed intentions

Clarity of Presentation
_____Defined new terms, concepts and principles
_____ Explicitly related new ideas to familiar ones
_____ Reiterated definitions of new terms as needed
_____ Used alternate explanations when necessary
_____ Slowed word flow when ideas were complex

Questioning Ability
_____Asked questions to see what attendees already knew about topic
_____ Used rhetorical questions to focus attention
_____ Paused after all questions to allow attendees time to think of an answer
_____ Encouraged attendees to answer difficult questions by question rephrasing
_____ Asked probing questions if responses were incomplete
_____ Repeated answers when necessary so that entire group could hear
_____ Refrained from answering question when unsure of correct response
_____ Requested that inappropriate questions be discussed outside of instructional session

*Adapted with permission from "Improving Your Lecturing," Nancy A. Diamond, Greg Sharp, and
John C. Ory of the Office of Instructional Resources, University of Illinois at Urbana-Champaign

Associations That Promote Bibliographic Instruction

The following is a selected list of associations that are relevant to bibliographic instruction programs. These associations are umbrella organizations equivalent to the division or subdivision that is appropriate for your individual interest. For example, within ALA there are divisions, such as the Association of College and Research Libraries(ACRL), with subsections, such as the ACRL-Bibliographic Instruction Section (BIS) and ACRL-Education and Behavioral Science Section (EBSS), that devote much time and energy to library instruction. In addition, there is a Library Instruction Round Table (LIRT), that is also concerned with improving bibliographic instruction in various settings. Comparable subgroups may be found in the associations listed below.

American Library Association (ALA)
50 East Huron Street
Chicago, IL 60611
312-944-6780
800-545-2433

American Association of Law Libraries (AALL)
53 West Jackson Boulevard, Suite 940
Chicago, IL 60604
312-939-4764

Association of American Law Schools (AALS)
1201 Connecticut Avenue, NW, Suite 800
Washington, DC 20026
202-296-8851

Catholic Library Association (CLA)
401 West Lancaster Avenue
Haverford, PA 19041
215-649-5250

Medical Library Association (MLA)
6 North Michigan Avenue, Suite 300
Chicago, IL 60602
312-419-9094

Special Libraries Association (SLA)
1700 18th Street, NW
Washington, DC 20009
202-234-4700

Electronic Bulletin Boards of Interest to Bibliographic Instruction Librarians

ALTLEARN@SJUVM. Alternative Approaches to Learning Discussion. Topics covered include: learning styles, facilitated communication, computer networks, autistic learning.
Bitnet: LISTSERV@SJUVM

ASSESS@UKCC. The discussion list covers assessment issues and policies as well as information on current practices in higher education. The purpose is to provide a forum for the exchange of ideas, models, resources and practical strategies on student assessment of learning and institutional effectiveness. Sample topics include developmental education, course selection, the costs of assessment programs and the assessment of needs of transfer students.
Bitnet: LISTSERV@UKCC
Internet: LISTSERV@UKCC.UKY.EDU

BI-L@BINGVMB. Bibliographic Instruction Discussion Group. This active list covers all aspects of bibliographic instruction: teaching methods, new technologies, cultural diversity, conceptual frameworks, announcements of relevant conferences, plus many other topics.
Bitnet: LISTSERV@BINGVMB
Internet: LISTSERV@BINGVMB.CC.BINGHAMTON.EDU

EDUTEL@RPIECS. Edutel's purpose is to consider how computer-mediated communication can be used to achieve educational goals. Sample topics include teaching via electronic mail, electronic term paper grading, virtual conferencing, and telecomputing in the classroom.
Bitnet: COMSERVE@RPIECS
Internet: COMSERVE@VM.ECS.RPL.EDU

LIBREF-L@KENTVM. Discussion of Library Reference Issues. Topics include traditional reference services, patron expectations, staff training, as well as the impact of CD-ROM and online searching on reference service.
Bitnet: LISTSERV@KENTVM
Internet: LISTSERV@KENTVM.KENT.EDU

MEDIA-L@BINGVMB. Media in Education. Topics covered have included classroom design, cyberspace, copyright, media centers, video and film contests, costs of various media set-ups, and lending and copying of media materials.
Bitnet: LISTSERV@BINGVMB
Internet: LISTSERV@BINGVMB.CC.BINGHAMTON.EDU

NEWEDU-L@VM.USC.EDU. New Paradigms in Education. The discussion list is concerned with the experimentation with and exploration of ways of educating. The list seeks answers to the questions, What are the new paradigms in education? and How can they be implemented?
Bitnet: LISTSERV@USCVM

PACS-L@UHUPVM1. Public-Access Computer Systems Forum. The University Libraries and the Information Technology Division of the University of Houston have established this list that deals with all computer systems that libraries make available to their patrons, including CD-ROM databases, computer-assisted instruction (CAI) programs, expert systems, hypermedia programs, library microcomputer facilities, local databases.
Bitnet: LISTSERV@UHUPVM1

TEACHEFT@WCU. Teaching Effectiveness. Though this was not a particularly active listserv in 1992, sample topics have included grading methods, centers for teaching methods, and assessment.
Bitnet: LISTSERV@WCU

TIPS@FRE.FSU.UMD.EDU. Teaching in the Psychological Sciences. Although the focus of this discussion group is primarily on teaching in the psychological sciences, it is open to anyone interested in exchanging ideas on teaching in general.
Bitnet: LISTSERV@FRE.FSU.UMD.EDU

Index